FAST
YOUR WAY TO
WELLNESS

FAST
YOUR WAY TO
WELLNESS

LEE HOLMES

MURDOCH BOOKS
SYDNEY · LONDON

CONTENTS

INTRODUCTION

**Welcome to a sensible, simple and sustainable approach
to intermittent fasting, featuring balanced meals made
using nutritious unrefined wholefoods to boost your energy.
Wholefoods typically contain fewer calories and more nutrients
than other foods, which means you can pile more onto
your plate and still maintain both your fast and a healthy diet.**

Intermittent fasting is a scientifically proven approach to achieving
health, longevity and sustainable weight loss. It involves reducing your
calorie intake from time to time (for example on two days each week)
to around 500 calories (2090 kilojoules) for women and 600 calories
(2510 kilojoules) for men. If you've been looking into intermittent fasting
for a while, I'm sure you will have spied the many available fasting
recipes for puddings, bakes and cakes that comfortingly have the
right number of calories but sadly are low in nutrients and sky-high in
processed and refined ingredients. These aren't the best types of foods
to feed your body if you're seeking lifelong health. I'm here to show you
that fasting can be healthy with the right food and ingredient choices,
and with recipes that not only taste fantastic but put you on the path
to good health and increased longevity. I'm also here to delight you with
the added bonus of hitting the magic number on your bathroom scales.

Including wholefoods means you don't have to drink copious amounts
of water and peck on birdseed, or live on low-calorie junk food on your
fasting days. Instead, you'll be able to eat well naturally and with a sense

Fasting can be healthy with the right food and ingredient choices, and with recipes that not only taste fantastic but also put you on the path to good health and increased longevity.

of abundance. You'll also meet your nutritional needs on your fasting days and derive the maximum amount of nutrition from every meal.

This book contains 85 fasting recipes to take you all the way from breakfast to dinner. They're all suitable for the intermittent fasting plan, which means you don't have to be a fully qualified calorie accountant to enjoy them. Fear not: you won't have to approach every meal as a maths assignment. All the hard work and measurements have been delegated to a select team of expert number-crunchers, allowing you to focus on your gastronomic choices and the deliciousness of the recipes. Crunch food, not numbers!

You'll discover several different fasting methods, so you can choose one that fits best with your lifestyle. You'll find information about the science of fasting, what it is, how it works and the enormous health benefits associated with it. You'll uncover tips on how to start your first fast, incorporate exercise into your routine, and monitor results and adjust as you go. There's a list of calorie counts that doubles as a shopping list, which will help you if you want to add certain ingredients to recipes or mix and match.

Flip over to the recipes now and have a look at all the yummy and easy-to-make creations you'll be enjoying with this book. Then head back here and be inspired to get started on your new voyage to wellness and weight loss.

PART 1

PUTTING INTERMITTENT FASTING INTO PRACTICE

HOW INTERMITTENT FASTING WORKS

Intermittent fasting with natural, unprocessed foods in a natural quantity and quality is a safe, commonsense and powerful way to achieve thriving health and vitality. It's far from a fleeting fad and is not new at all. Humans have been fasting for most of history for religious reasons (such as Lent, Yom Kippur or Ramadan), or during extended times of food scarcity experienced by hunter-gatherer societies. What *is* new is a growing body of clinical research backing the benefits of fasting.

We in the West have become snack-obsessed, thanks to marketing and an overabundance of food choices. Apart from when we're asleep, it's common for us to snack all day, giving our bodies little time to benefit from the healing and regenerative effects of fasting. With intermittent fasting you can 'bio-hack' your body, allowing it to reap the health benefits once enjoyed by hunter-gatherers, who ate only the foods provided by nature, and only *when* they were naturally and conveniently available.

Intermittent fasting is all about getting in sync with the natural biological processes and cues of *your* unique body. As a result of the industrial revolution and the globalisation of the modern food industry, our plates are filled with ingredients that our DNA may not be adapted to tolerate. Jumping off the continuous-eating bandwagon and incorporating regular bursts of fasting will allow you to rest, reset and regenerate your body, restoring its true functions.

Intermittent fasting is all about getting in sync with the natural biological processes and cues of your unique body.

Fasting will allow you to rest, reset and regenerate your body, restoring its true functions.

Intermittent fasting resets the body by helping it shift from a sugar-burning machine into a fat-burning machine. Refined grains and excess sugar form a large portion of the Western diet. These are broken down immediately into glucose and circulated in the bloodstream to fuel our bodies. Because the energy is readily available in our bloodstream, our body will use that energy rather than take it from any of our stores. Any excess glucose is converted and either stored as carbohydrate (glycogen) in the liver and muscles or as body fat. When we run out of glucose in our bloodstream, the body produces more by breaking down our glycogen stores, which we replenish every time we eat. This is a big problem, of course, for those needing to lose weight. Only when we enter the fasted state, where we have abstained from food for more than three hours, do we start to break down fat stores. Hello, weight loss!

Fasting also has a positive balancing impact on the hormones that govern our entire body, particularly those that control hunger and satiety. Insulin and leptin, two of these hormones, are highly influential in achieving homeostasis (stability) and fluidity in our wonderfully complex physiological systems. When these hormones are working properly, our body clearly informs us when to eat, when to store fat and when we need to increase our intake of carbohydrate for energy rather than fats or proteins. A modern diet rich in refined carbohydrates leads to overproduction of insulin and leptin at such a rate that they can exhaust and burn out their receptors, leading to a downward health spiral of inflammation, autoimmune conditions and chronic disease.

Scientific research into intermittent fasting is still in the early stages and so far has been mainly carried out on animal subjects, but there is no doubt that by abstaining from food for extended periods, or simply eating less twice a week, as I do, you'll consume fewer calories while limiting your intake of chemical additives and unhealthy foods. This alone will naturally yield improvements in a wide spectrum of general health and body composition indicators.

INSULIN AND LEPTIN

When the levels of glucose in our blood are high, our pancreas releases insulin, which triggers the body to store the glucose we don't need as glycogen. When we eat constantly, our insulin levels never fall, we develop insulin resistance and all that excess glucose remains in the blood, causing damage wherever it goes. This is the condition known as type 2 diabetes.

Our bodies are most sensitive to insulin following a period of fasting, making us more likely to use the food we consume more efficiently as energy. From an evolutionary perspective, our bodies are designed to flourish during fasting periods, burning fat stores for energy during times of famine, just like our hunter-gatherer ancestors. Fasting reprograms your cells so they derive most of your energy from fat. Depending on your unique constitution and current health, moving your body into this fat-burning state will take weeks, even months of intermittent fasting. This means that the key is to find a regular, sustainable fasting method that works for you and can be incorporated into your lifestyle with minimum fuss or disturbance.

Leptin, known as the 'master hormone', controls appetite, keeps our fat stores in the healthy range, and sends signals to the brain to inform us of fullness and satiety during meals. It is produced by our fat cells when they think we've had enough. Constant eating and not allowing the body to move into the fat-burning zone by timing meals sensibly increases the levels of leptin in our blood and our risk of developing leptin resistance. Lower levels of leptin in the blood are linked to a faster metabolism.

In combination, insulin and leptin resistance can lead to blood-sugar highs and lows, constant hunger, tiredness, thyroid problems, slow metabolism and even infertility.

THE HEALTH BENEFITS OF INTERMITTENT FASTING

Many of you will know that I was suffering from health issues and that I managed to restore myself to health, improving the symptoms of my fibromyalgia and autoimmune condition, through healing my digestive system. As my gut lining started to repair itself and my gut microflora (the population of good bacteria in my intestines) became balanced, many aspects of my health improved dramatically.

It's fascinating what an astoundingly accurate reflection of our emotional state our gut is. An unhealthy gut can bring us down, but if we take care of our digestive system, our emotions and mood will be affected in a positive way. For more on this and other aspects of gut health, please consult my book *Heal Your Gut* and the four-week online gut-healing programs on my website, superchargedfood.com.

If you want to feel great physically and emotionally, the first phase of looking after your gut and ensuring that it's performing optimally is giving it some downtime — let it lie on the couch, be in charge of the remote and relax. The next phase is nourishing it with organic, natural wholefoods; hydrating it with pure, filtered water and alkalising and nutrient-rich green juices; giving it a little boost with some probiotics and fermented foods; and supporting it by eating slowly and mindfully, chewing thoroughly, and keeping stress and negative emotions at bay.

Once your gut is in a healthy state, it's important to realise that, just like you, your digestive system sometimes needs a little rest and recuperation to be able to function at its best. That's when intermittent fasting can be really helpful. Think of fasting as a self-care practice, a much needed timeout for your gut for which your body and health will thank you. This isn't another fad diet or period of deprivation, and you're working within your own constitution and bodily systems.

In my book *Eat Right for Your Shape*, which is based on Ayurvedic principles, I introduce fasting recipes and benefits centred around increasing digestive fire (*agni*). I believe in the metabolism-boosting properties of a healthy meal during the period of highest digestion, so I eat my largest meal at lunchtime. On my fasting days, I try to eat dinner as early as possible to achieve double benefits, and I eat small quantities of nutrient-rich, easy-to-digest, seasonal foods suited to my dosha (personal energy type) during the 'feeding' phase. This lightens the load on my gut and prepares my body for a longer overnight fasting phase, to give my digestive system twelve to sixteen hours of total rest.

There are several approaches to intermittent fasting, as you'll see on page 20, but doing it twice a week, for example, will give your overworked digestive system some much-needed restorative time. It's just a case of eating fewer high-calorie processed foods and focusing on easy-to-digest wholefoods a couple of days a week. You can do this by following the recipes in this book. It's that simple.

Think of fasting as a self-care practice, a much needed timeout for your gut for which your body and health will thank you.

Apart from gut health, intermittent fasting has a range of regenerative and healing effects beyond its fat-burning benefits. Religions have long maintained that fasting is excellent for the soul, but its specific bodily benefits were only clinically recognised in the 1900s, when doctors recommended it to treat a multitude of disorders from diabetes to epilepsy. Research before 1945 and the advent of antibiotics and industrial pharmaceutical drug production highlighted the idea that periods of time without food reduced the risk of cancer and delayed the development of disorders that lead to death. It's only recently that researchers have begun to delve further into the age-old practice of intermittent fasting, with enlightening results.

Studies on mice have shown that periods of fasting protect the immune system from damage *and* induce immune system regeneration. Fasting may therefore have huge implications for the way we age, as immune system decline is a major contributor to disease and degeneration. During periods without food, the immune system responds by trying to save energy, so it recycles a lot of unused immune cells, especially those damaged by such things as ageing, chemotherapy, drugs and a toxic lifestyle. Fasting also lowers levels of insulin-like growth factor (IGF-1), a hormone linked to ageing, tumour progression and cancer risk.

Fasting may also hold the key to boosting brain health. Dietary restriction has been shown on experimental models of Alzheimer's disease, Parkinson's disease, Huntington's disease and stroke to pump up the resistance of neurons (nerve cells) in the brain to dysfunction and death. It does this by stimulating the acceleration of protein activity that suppresses oxidisation and the formation of free radicals.

Overall, research is beginning to point towards amazing cell-recycling and cell-regenerating mechanisms that are a direct result of intermittent fasting. This helps explain why, during times of sickness, we're less likely to want to eat – the fasting kicks our body into a mode of immune-cell sacrifice and regeneration, *upgrading* your immune system with the long-term goal of survival and vitality in mind.

CHOOSING THE
RIGHT FAST

Think of intermittent fasting as a lifestyle rather than a diet. It's always better to make a health practice part of your everyday life rather than apply a blanket set of strict rules that will only produce a short-term effect. You need to figure out a sustainable fasting protocol that you can weave into your own life and that will suit your gender, background, lifestyle and unique needs.

You may not be aware of it, but you're already doing intermittent fasting, alternating between periods when you don't eat (or eat less) and periods when you do. Every night, between the time you finish your dinner and the time you start breakfast, you're actually fasting. That's why breakfast is called break-fast.

In essence, it's about extending those fasting periods now and then to give your body a chance to regulate itself. You need to choose an approach that's flexible and works with your unique needs. You don't want anything too rigid that's just going to fall apart on you like a foolish faddish diet that omits whole food groups. There are many different intermittent fasting protocols, each with its own guidelines as to how long to fast and what to eat during the 'feeding' phase. Some experts, for example, advise abstaining from food for 24 hours at a time or even more, while others suggest eating only one meal on fasting days, at night. Some experts recommend fasting for two days every week (they call this 5:2), while others say that three days each week (4:3) will yield more significant results.

As long as women consume their 500 calories (2090 kilojoules) and men their 600 calories (2510 kilojoules) on fasting days, they can choose whichever approach suits them best. You can eat all your fasting-day calories in one meal or spread them between your meals throughout the day. This is a personal choice based entirely on your lifestyle considerations and individual needs. Ayurvedic practice leans towards eating three meals a day with no snacking, and eating your lightest meal at the end of the day and as early as possible.

You can fast on consecutive days or you can split them. You may tend to eat more on weekends, for example, and so fasting on Monday and Tuesday might suit; or you could be a shift worker and so consecutive days would work better for you. Alternatively, you might want to spread your fasting days out or swap days for greater flexibility. You can also experiment with mealtimes to discover what suits you best.

No method is right or wrong, so why not try out the various approaches detailed below and see which works best for you. The aim is to make it so easy that it becomes a regular practice. As with everything else, better results come with consistency and working within your own body's needs. If a certain approach seems too hard or mires you in a world of brain fog, that's your body telling you it's not the best way for you. Listen to your body and move slowly towards a workable solution.

TWO DAYS A WEEK

Two days of fasting each week is the magic number for positive effects on the appetite-regulating hormone leptin and to help you drop unwanted kilos. I fast (i.e. consume no more than 500 calories/2090 kilojoules) each Monday and Thursday, and have so far sustained this easily for three years. I've worked it into my life so it's part of my regular routine. I always look forward to fasting days because of the wonderful benefits I feel afterwards, such as a clear head and bountiful energy. I personally love breakfast and believe in the metabolism-boosting properties of a healthy brekkie within an hour or two of waking, after my yoga and meditation practice. I usually have a light breakfast, a very late lunch and an early light dinner. If I'm feeling hungry midmorning, I'll have a light snack such as sardines or steamed vegetables.

After some trial and error, I've found this to be the method that works best for my own body and lifestyle. You might find it easier, however, to skip breakfast because you're never that hungry in the morning anyway. Or you can pass on lunch so that you don't have to worry about taking a meal to work or wasting time in an overcrowded food court.

SKIPPING BREAKFAST

If you're a full-time worker or student, an intermittent fasting program that skips or delays breakfast is a great way to incorporate fasting into your daily life. This will free you up time-wise and give your digestive system a break in the morning. For the greatest effect, an overnight fast should be approximately sixteen hours long. If your last meal the previous day was at 7 pm, then this means a late breakfast or early lunch at 11 am.

With this fasting approach, you should eat normally and healthily – there's no need to restrict your calorie intake every day. The fasting time will do the work.

LIMITING EATING TO AN EIGHT-HOUR WINDOW

If you're a stay-at-home parent, if you work from home or if you have more of a routine weekly schedule, eating within an eight-hour window each day might be the easiest way for you to reap the benefits of intermittent fasting.

Here's how it might look:

- *Breakfast at 10 am*
- *Lunch at 2 pm*
- *Dinner at 6 pm.*

The times can be flexible depending on your personal schedule, as long as all your food consumption fits within an eight-hour time frame. This is a great way to both enjoy the healing benefits of intermittent fasting for your digestive system, and give your body the time it needs to fully metabolise your glycogen stores and move into fat-burning mode.

SUPERCHARGED TIP

The earlier you eat dinner, the greater the benefits on intermittent fasting days. Small quantities of nutrient-rich, easy-to-digest foods will lighten the load on your gut, and the overnight 'fasting' phase will be longer than usual, allowing your digestive system twelve to sixteen hours of complete rest.

This is a simple way to lose extra weight without depriving your body.

As for skipping breakfast, there's no need to restrict your calorie intake each day. Increasing your fasting time will do the work for you.

UP DAY, DOWN DAY

If your schedule is a little all over the place, a more flexible and irregular plan might work best for you. This method allows you to choose two or three days each week for more intentional fasting through restricting your eating window, then eat normally on the other days.

An up-and-down week might look like this:

- *Monday:* limit eating to an eight-hour window
- *Tuesday:* regular eating
- *Wednesday:* limit eating to an eight-hour window
- *Thursday:* regular eating
- *Friday:* limit eating to an eight-hour window
- *Weekend:* regular eating.

You might like to take it a little further by choosing carefully what you eat on limited-eating days, reducing your calorie intake by focusing only on liquids such as smoothies, juices, bone broths and soups, to really give your digestive system a break. In Ayurvedic nutrition, the ancient practice of fasting on kitchari – also known as partaking in a kitchari cleanse – is considered a fantastic purifying ritual. Kitchari, a porridge-like soup and staple comfort food of India, is calming and soothing to the digestive tract and warming to the body. In kitchari fasting, the body receives a limited range of foods, which requires it to produce fewer digestive enzymes, leading to easy digestion and cleansing of the body. You can do a kitchari cleanse at any time between fasts to further detoxify your body.

Alternatively, you might like to narrow the eight-hour window to a six-hour window. Try different variations and see which works best for you.

SUPERCHARGED TIP

Eggs, coconut oil and grass-fed
butter, eaten in small amounts,
will help you feel satiated and
do wonders for your body.

HORMONE-FRIENDLY INTERMITTENT FASTING FOR WOMEN

Traditional extended fasting can have a negative effect on female hormones, sending a signal that you're experiencing famine and triggering your body to shut down fertility. The most obvious manifestation of this is irregular or non-existent periods. Gentler intermittent fasting options allow women to experience the benefits of cellular clean-up and weight loss without jeopardising hormone function.

For women, an intermittent fasting program that includes quality saturated fats from foods such as eggs, coconut oil and grass-fed butter is vital to communicating to their body that it's in a safe environment for proper hormone synthesis. This will also ward off the brain fog, exhaustion, irritability and cold hands that can come with traditional fasting. It's doubly important to include these foods in order to avoid any unnecessary disordered eating patterns that can accompany calorie restriction and fat avoidance.

A safe fasting method for women would include fats at every opportunity. A late breakfast of poached eggs with avocado and spinach, followed by a midafternoon smoothie with coconut water and a vegetable and bone broth soup with a small amount of coconut oil or ghee for dinner is a nice gentle intermittent fasting option that will support hormone function while promoting weight loss and detoxification. Adding Celtic sea salt or Himalayan salt to filtered water and to meals will also do wonders.

TIPS TO STARTING YOUR FIRST FAST

Whenever you start something new, there are bound to be a few challenges, especially when it comes to something you do every day, like eating and drinking. If you're new to intermittent fasting, it's really important to set yourself up for the best start possible by being as organised and mentally prepared as you can. Intermittent fasting is *not* a quick-fix weight-loss solution, but a lifestyle choice that provides the greatest benefits when it becomes a long-term, sustainable practice. The last thing you want is for it to feel like a drag. Here are my master secrets, which you can implement for lasting fasting success!

CHOOSE AN APPROACH AND START SLOW

Take a realistic look at your lifestyle and make a decision about which method of fasting (see page 20) is right for you. If you've never fasted before, I highly recommend that you start slowly. Think of it initially just as a framework for controlling excesses. Progress gradually, one day at a time, until you're a full-blown intermittent-faster.

Perhaps for the first week choose to skip just one meal a day, and even replace it with a fresh vegie juice to begin with. Depending on how you respond, you could then replace it with only water or herbal tea. Experiment at first and learn what your body can handle. If you wig out, don't beat yourself up about it. Just try another approach until you find one that works for you.

HAVE A PLAN

Failing to plan is planning to fail. Being organised is one of the most important factors when carving out a healthy lifestyle. There are just too many variables that will throw you off track if you have no focus. If you don't own a diary and calendar, definitely invest in these – or use the apps on your phone or another device. Analyse each coming week. Do you have weddings or events where you want to get in on the eating? What are the best times for you to fast? How are you going to handle social situations where you may choose not to eat? (See page 53 for more on this.)

Once you've answered these important questions, create a sustainable and consistent plan for when you'll be fasting. Add reminders to your diary at appropriate times for writing shopping lists and restocking healthy ingredients. Make meal plans for the foods you'll be eating. Also add times for food preparation so you're never left empty-handed. You can take an afternoon each weekend, for example, to prepare your meals or their ingredients for the week to come.

FOCUS ON QUALITY FOOD

Intermittent fasting will bring the most health benefits and prove much more achievable if the food you consume around your fasting period is of the highest quality. Intermittent fasting shouldn't be a time of misery or deprivation – you should be able to take pleasure in the food you're consuming. Even during a fast, eating should always be a joyful experience rather than a chore.

Since you'll be eating less often, it's a good idea to invest in organic and at least chemical-free produce wherever possible. You'll find that eating grass-fed organic animal products and toxin-free produce will keep your body better nourished, keep you fuller for longer, and won't weigh your body down with chemicals. Instead of going to the supermarket for conventional produce, seek out local organic vegetable suppliers, farmers' markets or organic delivery services. Or try growing your own. Even in a flat you can grow herbs in a pot on a windowsill.

KEEP A JOURNAL

Dear diary ... Journalling can profoundly improve your wellbeing, and research shows that the practice of expressive writing strengthens immune cells and is associated with drops in depression and anxiety, and with increases in positive mood, social engagement and the quality of close relationships.

Fasting, in a spiritual sense, is also a time to enlarge and prioritise your soul. Food and the physical body govern so much of our life, but fasting is a time to put the physical aside and let your spiritual life expand. A little hunger therefore acts as a reminder to connect with your deeper world. For more on keeping a journal, see page 34.

DRINK WATER REGULARLY

Drink plentifully and proactively to ward off hunger. It's vitally important to stay hydrated during fasting periods, when you won't be able to obtain as much water from your food itself as you usually do. Your body will be doing lots of healing, regenerating and detoxifying, so you'll need adequate fluids to help fuel these processes. Always have a bottle of filtered water around you, or sip herbal tea throughout the day. Adding a pinch of Himalayan salt with dulse or nori flakes is a good way to balance out acidity, promote balance and flood the body with trace minerals. It's great for alleviating the odd hunger pang, too. Steer clear of low-cal drinks containing artificial sweeteners.

There's no such thing as a magic-potion supplement or drink that will give you lifelong sustained weight loss and health.

DON'T BE HARD ON YOURSELF

Always remember that intermittent fasting is not a diet. It's a healing practice that will reset and regenerate your body to a state of healthy balance. Don't place unrealistic expectations on yourself. Be mindful as you eat and mindful as you're not eating. Go over the health benefits on page 17 again if you have to, and while journalling create your own *why* behind your intermittent fasting journey (see page 34). Come back to that when the going gets tough, and stay focused. At the same time, never admonish yourself or feel guilty if you have a slip-up. Instead, get back to your *why* and keep on keeping on. Intermittent fasting shouldn't be stressful, but a peaceful and freeing habit.

If you want to lose weight but you don't do so after a few weeks or even months, don't lose heart. You body needs time to reset, and every day you eat healthily will always bring you a step closer to your health and/or weight-loss goals. Remind yourself that when it does happen, it will be a lasting change.

SUPERCHARGED TIP

Minimise stress on your body by
staying hydrated. Choose herbal
teas or brews that encourage
your body to cleanse itself.

HOW TO JOURNAL

⚓

Follow this guide to using a journal throughout your intermittent fasting voyage. Keep your journal on or inside your bedside table so it's easy to reach for at the end of each day. Create a regular quiet space in your day to write and reflect on your previous 24 hours. Write down the challenges you're facing, then make an action plan with solutions to help you navigate and stay the course. Jot down any symptoms you may be noticing. Write down and work through the emotions that come up during the fasting process. You need to express how you're *really* feeling, so vent your frustrations on the page. Monitor your results, and create a guide that you can reflect on and use as an impetus to make changes based on any patterns that arise. On day one of journalling, take a photograph and stick it in the inside front cover. That's the before shot!

1 FIGURE OUT THE *WHY* BEHIND YOUR QUEST FOR HEALTH

Put this on the very first page. What are your goals? Are they realistic? Do you want to lose weight? How much? Do you want to gain more energy? What improvements do you want to see in your life? And *why*? It's so important that your *why* comes from a place of love and respect for yourself. There's a big difference between striving for the physical perfection of a famous supermodel or a twiglet, and wanting to become a strong, healthy individual or parent and role model to your family. Take your *why* a little further by framing it as a short vision statement or mantra, and create a vision board in your journal as a visual reminder of what you want to achieve. Make intermittent fasting just one strategy you commit to in order to make this broader vision a reality.

2 BEGIN YOUR PLANNING

Map out the method of intermittent fasting you're going to attempt. Jot in the dates and times when you'll commit to fasting, and organise your meal plans, shopping lists and shopping times for the coming week. You'll need to do these planning sessions at the beginning of each new week.

3 WRITE A DATED JOURNAL ENTRY ONCE A DAY

Reflect on the previous 24 hours, and ask yourself these questions: How have I felt (physically and emotionally) in the last 24 hours? Is there anything I can change in my approach to better achieve my *why*? If weight loss is one of your goals, you might like to keep a weekly weight measurement and track your progress. Keeping a food diary alongside this will help you to reflect on the foods you've been consuming and assess whether they're serving your body or causing you to gain weight. The key with these kinds of recordings is not to become obsessive or negative. Remember to frame everything within your *why*, and be kind to yourself whatever the scales read.

4 FRAME EACH DAY WITH GRATITUDE

This is so important. If you can frame your intermittent fasting journey and goals with thankfulness and positivity along the way, you'll be much more likely to stay committed, and may even rewire some negative thought patterns about yourself along the way. Read the information on page 46 about rewiring your brain. Each day, commit to noting down ten things you're thankful for in your life. By the time you reach number seven, you'll find that any negative emotions regarding your self-image or pesky sabotaging thoughts will be crowded out by thankfulness, freeing you up to stay focused and in tune with your thoughts.

5 CREATE ACTION POINTS

If you discover that you need to make adjustments, be sure to include in your journal simple action points and reminders to move forward. You may find, for example, that a particular style of fasting continually clashes with your schedule. Your action point would need to include a realistic solution to this problem. You might even discover from your food diary that a particular food is consistently linked with certain unhealthy symptoms. In your action points you'd need to remind yourself not to include that food for the next week, and then to record at the end of that week if your symptoms cease. Use these action points in your weekly planning sessions to ensure you're continually growing, learning and refining your unique intermittent fasting protocol.

INTERMITTENT FASTING AND EXERCISE

To eat or not to eat, that is the question – especially when you're exercising. By now, you could be wondering about the benefits of running on empty – and I'm not referring to the Jackson Browne classic. There are quite a few different schools of thought, and a range of studies with different conclusions on how to approach exercise when engaged in an intermittent fasting protocol.

While you're in a fasted state, it's imperative that you listen to your body, take note of how you feel, and use these observations when considering how you'll approach exercise. That's rule number one. If it makes you feel terrible, listen to your body and don't do it until you're on a non-fasting day. If it makes you feel great, go for it, but in all cases the best thing is to check with your health practitioner before jumping into strenuous exercise. Crucially, what type of exercise you do, when you do it and how long for largely depends upon you. See how you feel and experiment with what works for your body – it could be slow movement such as walking, lower intensity weight training, beach jogging, yoga or Pilates. Once you're comfortable with a certain type of exercise, shorten your workouts and add bursts of higher intensity.

Research shows that exercising on an empty stomach will not nullify a workout but in fact can be very beneficial, as it triggers a cascade of hormonal changes throughout the body that are conducive to both building muscle and burning fat. When you're fasting, your body releases the hormone insulin less often, making it easier to burn fat and

improve blood flow to muscles. Intermittent fasting can also promote the release of human growth hormone, which helps the body make new muscle tissue, burn fat, and improve bone quality, physical function and longevity. Exercising while fasting can increase levels of testosterone, a hormone in both men and women that helps reduce body fat and increase muscle mass. The two hormones together are a magical pairing.

The easiest way to incorporate fasting exercise is to do some form of physical activity before breakfast. The early morning is the best time for exercise, particularly as the sun is low on the horizon in those earlier hours. The angle of the sunlight to your eyes stimulates the pituitary gland, which regulates hormones, releases endorphins and sets up your circadian rhythms.

HIGH-INTENSITY INTERVAL TRAINING

Some health experts advocate combining intermittent fasting with high-intensity interval training (HIIT), or short intense bursts of activity during the fasted state. They see the two as a powerful combo to turbocharge weight loss and promote the growth of quality fast-twitch muscle fibres that are increasingly resilient to oxidative stress. Burn, baby, burn!

Studies show that combining fasting with HIIT triggers the production of growth factors that signal brain stem cells to convert into new neurons and stimulate muscle satellite cells to convert into new muscle cells. This is, in effect, a recycling and upgrading process within your tissues that helps keep your muscle fibres biologically young. It is, in fact, a negative-feedback loop (see page 49).

This approach, however, is better suited to men and bodybuilders than most women. A woman's body is much more likely to produce a negative hormonal response when, from an evolutionary perspective, it believes it's suffering simultaneous physical stress and absence of food. HIIT with intermittent fasting could potentially put too much strain on a woman's hormonal health and fertility. If you'd like to exercise on fasting days, I'd recommend speaking to your health practitioner first. You should also start with gentler exercise during fasting periods, and work your way up to more intense activity if your body seems to respond well. If you begin to experience exhaustion, mental fog, mood swings,

irregular periods, irritability or tiredness, take that as a sign that
you need to take it easier on fasting days.

For both sexes, combining HIIT and intermittent fasting requires
careful timing of exercise and protein replenishment to achieve the
desired muscle-regenerative outcome. The last thing you want when
exercising in the fasted state is for your body to start breaking down
muscle for energy. Promote recovery from exercise by feeding your
muscles with fast-assimilating protein foods such as yoghurt or cheese
within 30 minutes of exercising. A pre-exercise fast improves the
absorption of a post-workout meal.

*Intermittent fasting exercise
has longer lasting benefits, as
the body gets used to using
its energy stores and learns to
exert itself in a fasting state.
This means that your body's
performance and quality
improve when it does have juice
in the tank on non-fasting days.*

SLOWING DOWN CRAVINGS DURING FASTING

Some days, ice cream is going to call from the fridge and you'll be daydreaming of a date with an iced doughnut with rainbow sprinkles. Without the right strategies, your cravings will drive you. If you're plagued by constant and obsessive food thoughts, thankfully there are several things you can do to stop cravings in their tracks and even prevent them happening in the first place.

LEAN INTO YOUR CRAVINGS

It's most likely a valid signal that your body is in need of particular nutrients. Make sure you assess what your body is telling you. Here are some common craving signals with solutions to overcome them. Depending on your fasting method, you may be able to consume some of these foods during a craving, but if you can't, make sure you're getting these foods during times of non-fasting.

If you have a craving for:

- oily or fried foods – top your body up with some extra virgin coconut oil, cold-pressed extra virgin olive or macadamia oil, avocado, or oily fish such as salmon or sardines. One teaspoon of oil contains about 40 calories (170 kilojoules), so don't be afraid to drizzle a little on your meals during fasting days.
- starchy carbs – satisfy your carb craving by adding a small sweet potato (86 calories/360 kilojoules per 100 grams), swede

SUPERCHARGED TIP

For days when you're too tired to cook from scratch, about 1 cup (250 ml/9 fl oz) of healthy ready-made fresh soup or sashimi, seaweed and edamame will weigh in at under 200 calories (840 kilojoules).

(rutabaga) (38 calories/159 kilojoules per 100 grams), parsnip (75 calories/314 kilojoules per 100 grams) or piece of butternut pumpkin (squash) (45 calories/188 kilojoules per 100 grams) to your meals.

- sugary sweets – reconsider fake sugars or low-carb products, including beverages, because they don't quell cravings and can have unpleasant side effects. Seek out low-fructose and low-calorie fruits such as berries, apple, pineapple, kiwi fruit or grapefruit. Sprinkle ground cinnamon and stevia on apple slices for a delicious snack.
- salty snacks – drink a big glass of water with ⅛ teaspoon Celtic sea salt or Himalayan salt to both fill you up and restore your salt balance.
- food in general – cut up a bunch of vegetables, put slices or batons in individual bags and store them in the fridge ready for when cravings hit.

KEEP BUSY

Plan your intermittent fasting days for when you know you won't be home, sitting on the couch on a slow-drag rainy Tuesday, being tempted by a virtual conveyor belt of unhealthy snacks. Pick your fasting days for when you're busy at work or running errands and you'll be less likely to be daydreaming about food. Don't plan to fast when you know you have a family gathering or social event, or you might find yourself crash-tackling a relative to get to the fondue fountain or buffet.

KEEP YOUR BLOOD SUGAR STABLE

If you have periods of low energy, moodiness or the jitters, it might be wise to eat a good breakfast, and include protein with every meal to stabilise your blood sugar when fasting.

SWEETEN UP

If you're craving sweetness, then instead of bingeing or thinking negative thoughts, add something sweet to your life so you can operate from a place of abundance and overflow. Nourish yourself with loving thoughts and self-care practices so that you feel rested, strong and complete. Indulge in a massage, see a movie or take a long relaxing bath. It's a simple shift, but it will slow your cravings and allow you to feel nurtured.

GET AN EARLY NIGHT

Take the opportunity to get to bed earlier and use the time for restoration of your body. Saving calories for your main meal in the early evening can also help you sleep and will make you less likely to awake with the sleep hungries at 2 am. Establishing a sleep routine that helps you prepare for bed can help. It could be making a herbal tea, brushing your teeth, taking a stroll around the block after dinner or reciting your favourite quote or poem. If you still can't sleep, repeat the process.

REMOVE THE FOCUS FROM WEIGHT LOSS

While weight loss is a natural consequence and pleasing side effect of intermittent fasting, it's also a tricky business. Setting it up as your sole purpose and focus will make willpower your fallback position every time. It's far better to channel your energy towards understanding your behaviours and motivations at their origin, and using what you've learnt about yourself to bring about a meaningful change in your health and wellbeing.

TAKE A MENTAL VACAY

If none of these seem to work, and that dreaded bowl of cheesy fries is relentlessly taunting you, take a mental vacation by going for a walk in nature. Research from Dr Jon May and his team at Plymouth University's Cognition Institute in the United Kingdom shows that distraction uses mental processes similar to cravings, so distracting yourself is particularly good at making cravings easier to resist. If you find walking too dull, you could instead distract yourself with a good book, an engaging TV series, a visit to an art gallery or a yoga class. When you switch gears, you take the focus off what you don't have and enjoy the moment instead.

ONLY BREAK GLASS IN CASE OF EMERGENCY

TWELVE TIPS FOR SURVIVING FASTING DAYS

⚓

When you're being clobbered
by cravings, use these
'distraction actions' to stop
cravings in their tracks:

1
Drink two glasses
of water right now.

2
Light an aromatic
vanilla candle and
take a breath.

3
Put on a five-star
track and dance around
the room, working on
your disco moves.

4
Keep busy. Clean out
a cupboard or untangle
power cables.

5
Reach out via email or
phone to a friend you
haven't spoken to for a
while, or join an online
forum for support.

6
Make a mental list
of five reasons
you're fasting.

7
Choose a reward for
tomorrow – it need
not involve food.

8
Take a belfie (belly selfie)
and compare it to one
after a day of fasting.

9
Treat fasting day as
a self-care day, with a
bath and an early night.

10
Outsmart cravings
by brushing
your teeth.

11
Do three-part breathing:
fill your belly, then fill your
lower ribcage, then fill
your upper chest with air
in one slow breath, then
slowly release the air.
Repeat ten times.

12
Surf the urge
and wait it out.
Hang tough!

REWIRE YOUR BRAIN

You don't have to react to every single one of your thoughts. Your mind will tell you a million things you need to do each day, but it's not always the truth. Our brains are very good at sabotaging our own goals, especially when there's a root fear of failure or a victim mentality deep within us. But our brains are also remarkably malleable. If you find that negative thought patterns arise, recognise that you're trying to do something good for your health and that with any sacrifice comes challenge. Don't try to overcompensate with extra deprivations if you've caved in to a craving. Self-revenge will only make the situation worse and create more negative self-talk.

A study published in *Psychology and Health* in 2012 followed three groups of chocolate-cravers who were made to carry around a bag of chocolate for seven days and try to resist eating it. One group was simply left to deal with carrying around the chocolate on their own. They were the control group, used to compare with the other two groups. The second group was taught to use cognitive restructuring techniques. These involved identifying problematic thinking about cravings, rationally addressing each craving, and then coming up with new thoughts to reframe the situation. Fundamentally, this kind of strategy involves self-evaluation and coming up with your own defensive thinking to remove the negative thought.

The third group used cognitive defusion techniques, which change the function of negative thoughts rather than try to modify their content as cognitive restructuring does. Cognitive defusion involves speaking or writing out negative thought patterns repeatedly until they lose their meaning. They can then be observed for what they are – often a mistruth – and the person with the craving can move forward.

The study showed that the chocolate-cravers who used cognitive defusion techniques were more than three times more likely to resist eating the chocolate. Essentially, 'trying' to fix the thought patterns that come with cravings is less successful than simply acknowledging and speaking out your negativity.

Incorporating some cognitive defusion techniques will help you overcome cravings during your fast. You can do this by journalling (see page 34) or simplifying your negative feelings to one word and repeating it aloud. It might be 'starving' or 'deprived'. Just 20–30 seconds of quick repetition of this word has been proven to reduce the emotional discomfort and believability of your negative thought. You may find that the bad feelings you're experiencing are far more exaggerated than the reality of your situation, which will free you up to stay the course.

Always speak to yourself as a loving friend would. Tell yourself 'I can do this' and learn how to roll with the punches. Treat yourself with care and kindness, and if you slip up and accidentally take a trip to the corner shop for chocolate biscuits, corn chips, jelly snakes and other childhood friends, just forgive yourself – don't let guilt and regret get the better of you. Accept yourself, then get back on track with positivity and realistic expectations. Healthy eating is all about balance and moderation.

Speak your truth
or forever hold
your peas!

COMMON FASTING-DAY PROBLEMS AND SOLUTIONS

THE PROBLEM **THE FIX**

Hunger scares you. ⟿ *Challenge your fear by telling your hunger to 'bring it on'.*

You're still gobbling up garbage. ⟿ *Stick to nourishing foods in an unprocessed state.*

You're drinking coffee to keep you going. ⟿ *Drink dandelion tea or another herbal tea in its place.*

You're not keeping occupied. ⟿ *Schedule activities so you're not idle.*

You're consuming low-calorie junk food. ⟿ *Choose wholefoods from the earth.*

You're overcomplicating things. ⟿ *Keep it simple by getting back to basics.*

Deprivation makes you anxious. ⟿ *Know that negative-feedback loops and periods of deprivation allow the body to reset itself and reach a state of balance (see opposite).*

HARNESS NEGATIVE-FEEDBACK LOOPS

Despite their name, these can be a very positive thing. Negative feedback happens when a stimulus causes an opposite output in a system and this regulates that system to return it to an ideal level. Think of it as an extremely complex balancing act. Imagine two opposing forces operating in balance. When one of them overtakes the other and the system gets out of kilter, that influence feeds back into the system and increases the effect of the opposing force. In human biology, this process is known as reaching homeostasis. In the physical world, it's referred to as achieving equilibrium.

Widely used in mechanical and electronic engineering, negative-feedback systems can occur naturally, both in the physical world and within living organisms such as humans. Once you know how to recognise them, you'll start seeing them everywhere.

Think, for example, about water flowing through a fracture in a rock. Eventually it deposits enough sediment to slow down the flow of the water. Or about how plants increase their rate of photosynthesis when levels of carbon dioxide are high. This uses up the carbon dioxide and produces more oxygen, bringing the gases back into equilibrium. Or how about when you're reprimanded for coming in to work late, and the next day you come in fifteen minutes early? Or at university, say, when we get some exam questions wrong, and it prompts us not to make the same mistake next time? It happens in sport when a coach explains weaknesses in the team's defence.

Negative-feedback loops help keep our body temperature at a constant 37°C (99°F). If we become too hot, the blood vessels in our skin enlarge, enabling us to lose heat and cool down. If we get too cold, the blood vessels in our skin become smaller, allowing us to lose less heat and warm up our bodies. At the same time, if the temperature drops, our body shivers, resulting in an increase in temperature, while if it's too warm, our body sweats to initiate evaporative cooling.

But how, you might ask, does this relate to intermittent fasting? Four major negative-feedback loops have been identified that reveal why fasting benefits the body, promotes longevity and protects against disease:

1. Fasting increases insulin sensitivity (see page 15), making us more likely to use the food we consume more efficiently and increasing energy efficiency within each cell. This slows down ageing and reduces the risk of disease.

2. Fasting decreases the accumulation of oxidative free radicals in cells, thus preventing oxidative damage to cells.

3. Fasting induces cells to increase the expression of genes that intensify our ability to cope with stress.

4. Fasting makes the body self-regulate to boost nutrient uptake, making it even more efficient.

When negotiating with cravings, always remember that difficulties faced mean bigger rewards. You'll get through this.

USE ACUPRESSURE

Did you know you have magic fingers that can home in on acupressure points in your body to reduce food cravings? The next time you have an attack of the munchies, try massaging one of these acupuncture points for several minutes before eating, to help reduce hunger and control your appetite.

Place your index finger next to the small piece of flesh that protrudes from the inside of your ear, just above the earlobe. This is the primary appetite-control point. Hold this part of the ear between your thumb and index finger, and manipulate for three minutes with a medium amount of pressure.

Or place your thumb and index finger on the knobbly spot just behind and beneath your earlobe, right behind where the earlobe meets the skin near the jaw. It feels very relaxing to touch. Massage for one to three minutes.

Directly between the upper lip and the nose lives another major appetite-control point. It's about one-third of the way down from the bottom of the nose. Apply moderate pressure to this area with your index finger and manipulate it for a minute or two.

THE SOCIABLE FAST

Your social life will be one of the greatest variables in the success of your fast, so it's crucial that you wrap your head around how you'll wrangle it.

Sharing food in a social setting is one of life's greatest joys, but if you're trying to stick to a particular style of eating, it can be really challenging to speak up about your choices. You may feel afraid of what people will think of you and that you might be judged by your friends as a party pooper or a freakish activated nut.

It's really important again to reflect on the *why* behind your fasting and ask yourself: is this goal more important than eating whatever's on offer at this birthday party? If it isn't, then you might like to strengthen your *why* into a greater goal that has more significance for your life. It's so important to have a strong mindset from the beginning, or every wedding or staff birthday cake will be another variable to take you off course. Rehearsing a little line in your head that can be used in social situations to explain why you're skipping dessert is also a great preparation that will save any awkward moments.

Celebrations should be the time when you eat something rather than nothing. If you're going to be at a wedding or important event, save your fasting for another day. Or if you really want to stick to your routine, include your requirements in your RSVP – but bear in mind how inconvenient this could be for the event planners.

If you're planning on going out to a restaurant for dinner, you can call them and ask if they can make any adjustments for you. Restaurants are used to doing this and will be even happier to alter their menu if they're expecting you.

When ordering food at a cafe or restaurant, you can almost always guarantee that they'll offer steamed vegies and salads. Ask for steamed vegetables on their own or with grilled chicken, fish or meats, with no seasonings or sauces. Order salads with no dressing but with a squeeze of lemon if they have it. Instead of breads for starters, ask for some olives. For dessert, request fresh fruit or a pot of herbal tea. If the food is going to be share platters, do your best to pick out little bits that you can eat, and eat very slowly and mindfully, so you don't overdo it.

When you can, try to be the friend who recommends something different for a celebration or social gathering. Suggest a potluck picnic where you can bring your own food and drink to share, or go for a big long walk or an op-shop crawl rather than a standard cafe catch-up. There are so many other ways to spend time with friends that will enrich and add more depth to your relationships.

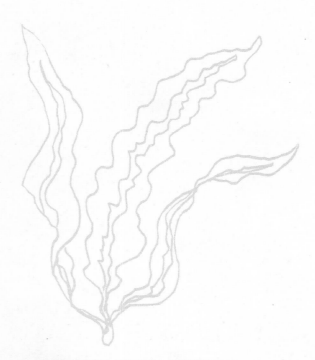

SUPERCHARGED TIP

When going out for coffee, stick to fresh vegetable juices or herbal teas, or seek out local juice bars or organic cafes that offer a range of fast-friendly options.

A FASTING PANTRY

There's nothing more satisfying than opening your fridge and cupboards to a display of fresh ingredients that are organised and easy to access – and nothing worse than a chaotic labyrinth of who-knows-what lurking in the pantry. Here are some savvy tips to fastify your kitchen and make your fasting days as undemanding as possible.

CLEAN OUT THE JUNK

Go through every item in your pantry and fridge. Bin anything that's past its use-by date, and give away or recycle anything with an ingredients list that includes additives, flavourings, artificial colours or anything with a number in it. You really want to eliminate packaged foods as much as possible, unless they contain 100 per cent real food ingredients that Great Grandma or Grandpa would recognise. Make it your aim to have a 'one-ingredient pantry', where everything is a single spice, herb, grain or other food item. Avoid anything that has been conveniently combined in a package with a range of different foods and additives.

PLAN AHEAD

Figure out your meal plan for the week ahead and plot when you'll be cooking and eating specific recipes. Make a note of everything from breakfast to dinner, including any herbal teas or snacks you may like to have on hand. This way you'll fill your kitchen with everything you need, without any budget-breaking, waste-making purchases. Note the days you'll be fasting and you'll need fresh produce.

KNOW YOUR SUPPLIERS

Before refilling your kitchen with an array of gorgeous food, it's a great idea to consider local producers, markets, organic food suppliers, co-ops and services that offer the best price and the best quality ingredients before you go out on your shopping spree. Do some web surfing and make some phone calls. Ask about the quality of the produce. Ask about pesticides, organic certification, and whether the meat is organic and 100 per cent grass-fed, grass-finished and free from antibiotics. You might like, for example, to buy your meat from a local organic butcher, vegetables from a farmers' market, and bulk nuts and seeds from an organic wholefoods store or co-op. Figure out what's best for you, your budget and your health. Not everything needs to be organic if it doesn't fit in with your budget or lifestyle – health is also about balancing what is and isn't achievable. Try not to remove whole food groups from your diet unless you need to for medical reasons.

WRITE A PRECISE SHOPPING LIST

Once you've planned your meals and know your suppliers, write a heading for each supplier on a sheet of paper, and then use your meal plan and recipes to note under the appropriate heading every single item needed to make those recipes. This will revolutionise the productivity of your household food-gathering, but you'll need to be very thorough so as not to miss out on any ingredients and avoid those annoying last-minute trips to the shops. This will also ensure you're always prepped for fasting days, setting you up for a landslide victory.

NOTE YOUR PREP

Finally, you'll need to make time in your diary for food preparation. Do you need to make non-moo nut milks or bone broths? Are there times you'll be too busy to cook dinner, requiring a batch-cooking session beforehand? Note all these subtleties in your weekly diary, so your meal planning flows rather than being a burden. Use the calorie counters and meal plans on pages 86–105 as a guide.

SUPERCHARGED TIP

Remember to have on hand lots of fresh foods, including fruit and vegetables, the day before a fasting day, so you can reach for a healthy bite when needed.

WHAT TO EAT ON
NON-FASTING DAYS

My intermittent fasting program isn't designed to be the type of burdensome project on specific days of the week that makes 'off days' an excuse for a junk-food extravaganza. This program has to be approached holistically, with every day of the week in mind. It will work best when you honour your body every single day and take a balanced and moderate approach.

Your aim on the days when you're not fasting should always be to fill your body with a range of nutrient-dense wholefoods that serve your unique biochemistry. If you have food sensitivities or intolerances, you'll need to make sure you're filling any gaps with potentially lost nutrients. Always opt for foods in their most natural state, and buy additive-free and organic products wherever possible.

Here are some of the foods I'd recommend to achieve a state of thriving health in the long term.

LOTS AND LOTS OF PLANTS

Health advocates never butt heads on the value of eating loads of plants, particularly vegetables. This is your best health insurance. Dark leafy greens such as spinach, silverbeet (Swiss chard), rocket (arugula) and kale should be highest on your priority list, as they're dense in nutrients that fight chronic disease and in chlorophyll, which oxygenates the blood, increases energy and detoxifies the whole system.

I aim to eat from the rainbow every day: buckets of greens and a selection of orange, red, yellow and purple vegetables to provide me with a range of different antioxidants that function in different health-protective ways. Be sure to eat a balance of raw and cooked vegetables. You shouldn't be afraid of cooking your vegies. In fact, cooking breaks down the cell walls of vegetables to make many nutrients more bio-available, and cooked food is much easier on your digestive system.

As for fruits, try to make the majority low-fructose fruits that won't spike your insulin levels. Berries of all kinds are wonderfully delicious and bursting with free-radical-fighting properties. Kiwi fruit, pineapple, cranberries, apricots, lemons, limes and grapefruit are lower in fructose and provide a beautiful hit of vitamin C your body will love.

A RANGE OF QUALITY PROTEINS

Protein provides amino acids that are vital to the structural integrity of your entire body. It's really important to try to consume protein with every meal in order to keep your blood-sugar levels stable and promote satiety. When planning your meals, you should always envisage the entire week so you can include a range of proteins rather than eating chicken six times a week.

Over each week I like to include an organic chicken meal, an organic grass-fed beef or lamb meal, a wild-caught fish meal (salmon, sardines, cod or halibut) for omega-3 fatty acids, and a strategic combination of pulses, nuts, seeds and grains to create a complete protein.

Some combinations of plant foods that create a complete protein include:

- nuts and seeds with grains – such as macadamia nuts, almonds, chia seeds or pepitas (pumpkin seeds) with oats, buckwheat, rice or quinoa;
- nuts and seeds with legumes – such as cashew nuts, almonds, walnuts, sunflower seeds or sesame seeds with lentils, peas or beans;
- grains with legumes – such as quinoa, millet, rice, corn or oats with lentils, peas or beans.

HIGH-QUALITY FATS

Fat is no longer a dirty word in nutrition circles. In fact, saturated fat is now recognised as incredibly important for brain health, proper nerve signalling, hormone synthesis and fertility, while monounsaturated fats are crucial for regulating blood-sugar levels, maintaining healthy cholesterol levels and preventing heart disease. It's the polyunsaturated fats in processed vegetable oils that you want to avoid.

I like to consume my saturated fats from cuts of 100 per cent grass-fed and grass-finished red meat, free of hormones, pesticides and antibiotics. Organic is always best. Cold-pressed extra virgin coconut oil is another wonder ingredient high in saturated fats that also provides antimicrobial benefits to your gut, knocking out bad bacteria and keeping the good guys in balance.

For monounsaturated fats you should regularly consume cold-pressed olive oil, avocados, and activated nuts and seeds. For omega-3 fatty acids, go for cold-pressed flaxseed oil, and consume sustainable wild-caught fish such as sardines and salmon a couple of times a week. These will boost brain health and cognitive function, and provide a range of anti-inflammatory benefits.

SUPERCHARGE YOUR SEASONINGS

Never underestimate the power of a little seasoning. Dried and fresh herbs and spices punch well above their weight in terms of medicinal benefits and nutrient density. Always keep your kitchen full of fresh herbs or grow them yourself. Sprinkle them into and over everything to get a phytonutrient and antioxidant boost. Keep dried spices like cardamom, cinnamon, cloves and turmeric to sprinkle into soups, stews and slow-cooker meals.

Salt is also critical for keeping your body on an even keel. Try to avoid conventional iodised salt depleted of trace minerals, which is often tainted with nasty anti-caking ingredients. Quality Celtic sea salt or Himalayan salt is one of your greatest investments. To pump up the iodine you can combine it with dulse seaweed flakes for a natural iodised salt.

SUPERCHARGED TIP

If you ever want to dry your own home-grown or store-bought herbs you haven't used fresh, tie the stems together with string and hang them upside down somewhere in your kitchen for a week or until dry. Shake the leaves off and store them in jars for use in cooking.

PORTION CONTROL

As part of the moderation revolution, you must pledge to maintain portion control. You can still enjoy nourishing food during periods of intermittent fasting, but your focus will be on both the quality and quantity of your serving, and knowing the types of food to minimise or increase. Use this navigation guide to help you control your portions, but don't implement it in a micromanagement kind of way. You have the freedom to consult it when you feel you need to.

DRINK WATER

Drinking water ten minutes before a meal is a simple but effective way to ensure you're only eating what your body needs. So often our brain mistakes thirst for hunger, and without adequate hydration we're much more likely to overload our plate. Drinking water regularly throughout the day will boost your metabolism, cleanse your body of toxins and suppress hunger. Try to aim for around eight glasses a day.

LOAD UP ON VEG

Non-starchy vegetables are another easy way to fill yourself up without weighing your digestive system down. The good thing about vegetables is that they're low in calories but extremely high in micronutrients and fibre. They'll cleanse, detoxify and heal your body, and are very easy to digest. During fasting times, vegetables such as spinach, fennel, lettuce, green beans, cucumber, onions, broccoli, zucchini (courgettes) and asparagus should take up the largest proportion of your plate.

USE A SMALLER PLATE

Research has proven that larger plates make food portions seem smaller, while smaller plates make a meal seem bigger. This optical illusion can make all the difference to whether we feel deprived or blessed. Switch your regular large plate to something smaller, to keep your brain grateful and ward off negative feelings of scarcity.

USE CARBS AS A GARNISH

Avoid making carbohydrate-rich foods such as fruit, grains and starchy ingredients like potatoes the centre of a meal. Always base your meals on non-starchy vegetables and think of carbs as a topper rather than the star of the show. This is really important for keeping your blood-sugar levels stable, minimising inflammation in the body and moving your body into the fat-burning zone.

EAT MINDFULLY

Eating mindfully firstly involves being mindful about your attitude towards food. The ritual of saying grace before a meal far pre-dates its modern context, and is one of the most universal behaviours for a reason. Expressing thankfulness before a meal brings a sense of gratitude and wipes out negative emotions surrounding food. It acts as a kind of psychological purification, and studies show that this enhances our entire wellbeing, reduces stress and brings us greater life satisfaction.

SLOW IT DOWN

Eating with a mindful, grateful spirit also involves slowing down to savour the meal rather than shovelling it in at lightning speed. This is much better for your digestion and nutrient uptake. Sit down to eat.

Dawdle and enjoy. Pause between mouthfuls and put your fork down, allowing your body to take in the flavours and nourishment slowly. You can also minimise your food intake by consuming things that have a shell or peel, such as mandarins, edamame (soya beans in their pods), pistachios or walnuts. There is something quite meditative about cracking through nuts one by one, and you'll really relish their goodness.

ENJOY THE PREP

Much of the enjoyment of eating actually comes from the preparation, but unfortunately we live in a world where we're all about the quick fix. I'd really encourage you to get involved in the preparation of your food from soil or plot to plate. Enjoy selecting, preparing and then consuming your food. When you're aware of where it has come from and the efforts you and others have put in to bringing it to your table, you'll be incredibly thankful for even a small serving.

SUPERCHARGED TIP

Change your thoughts: think of fasting as a self-care practice, a needed timeout for your gut for which your body and health will thank you. This is *not* another fad diet or period of deprivation.

FASTING STAR
INGREDIENTS

Fasting encourages mindful eating, so stocking your pantry and fridge with healthy low-cal food will make your fasting days seem effortless and stop you climbing the walls with hunger. Opt for vibrantly coloured food that's bursting with flavour.

When you have lots of fresh ingredients on hand, it's much easier to cook from scratch and enjoy variety. As in non-fasting times, aim for plenty of fresh wholefoods and vegetables, good-quality protein and small amounts of high-quality carbohydrate. Cut out artificial sweeteners, sugars and inflammatory polyunsaturated fats. Fresh seasonal produce is the most satisfying and best value. If you have time, prepare your meals in advance, to avoid grazing while cooking.

If you're fasting on the same meals each week, it's easy to get bored and slip up, so try new foods each week to avoid getting into a rut. Here are some perfect fasting foods to try.

STEAMED FISH

Steamed fish is a light, nutrient-dense fasting food. Oily fish such as sardines or salmon will give you a hit of omega-3 and other long-chain fatty acids. Ocean-caught white fish such as flathead or snapper is delicious when steamed and eaten with a squeeze of lemon. Look for sustainable wild-caught fish. Try Wrapped Fish Peperonata (page 216).

BUCKWHEAT

Buckwheat isn't technically a grain but the seeds of a herb. It's high in the amino acid lysine, as well as calcium, vitamin E and the entire vitamin B complex. This traditional Russian staple is most digestible when sprouted by rinsing twice a day for one to three days, then dehydrating or dry-roasting in a frying pan before making into delicious porridges or breads. You'll love Orange and Cinnamon Buckwheat Porridge (page 119).

BONE BROTHS

Slowly simmered stocks made using fish, lamb, chicken or beef bones are extremely nutritious. They contain a range of immunity-boosting minerals – including calcium, magnesium and potassium – as well as gelatine, which is known for its gut-healing properties. These valuable broths can be frozen for weeks. Consume them as a nourishing low-cal beverage or use them to make stews, soups or sauces.

EDAMAME

These are young soya beans, still in their pods. Simply steamed in sea-salted water, the peeled green beans make a delicious snack that are an excellent source of plant-based protein, fibre, iron and vitamins C and K. Eating them from the pod takes time, which will slow down the amount you consume and keep calories to a minimum.

SASHIMI

Sashimi is thin slices of raw fish. Although home-made is always best, if you're ever in need of a quick takeaway lunch or dinner, sashimi is a good option. Sashimi is low in calories and high in omega-3 fatty acids and protein, which means it will fill you up without weighing you down.

LEAFY SALAD GREENS

Leafy greens will never weigh you down, and they'll flood your body with micronutrients and chlorophyll that will give you a hit of energy during fasting slumps. Baby English spinach, cos (romaine) lettuce and rocket (arugula) are more nutrient-dense than the standard iceberg lettuce and are still easy to eat raw in a salad.

HERBAL TEAS

If you need a little something sweet during your fast, or you're feeling a little deprived, a herbal tea is the perfect pick-me-up. Make it a mindful ritual using some pretty china, and it will satisfy something deeper as an act of self-care. Dried herbs such as peppermint, chamomile, licorice root, fennel or dandelion are highly cleansing and calming for your digestive system. You can also make teas using fresh ingredients, such as sliced ginger, turmeric or citrus fruit, rosemary and thyme.

CAPSICUMS

Capsicums (peppers) are a beautiful source of vitamin C, and make an aesthetically pleasing and sweet addition to salads and cooked meals. Slice them raw to enjoy with dips, or make a fast-friendly meal by halving them, stuffing them with vegetables, fish or other low-calorie ingredients and grilling them. Capsicum Cups (page 245) make a nutritious and filling lunch.

BANANAS

This common yellow staple is a great one to keep in your bag as a pep-me-up. Conveniently packaged and high in vitamins B6 and C, magnesium, potassium and fibre, bananas even contain a little protein. They're very easily digested and light on the tummy. Eat them raw, frozen and blended into smoothies, or sliced on your morning muesli or porridge. Blend with eggs and enjoy perfect Banana Pancakes with Blueberries (page 129).

EGGS

Eggs have provided humans with high-quality protein and fat-soluble vitamins for millennia. They're quick and easy to prepare as omelettes or scrambles, or simply poached or boiled. Buy the best quality eggs you can find – organic or from your local farmers' market – which will have a better fatty-acid profile and a lovely dark-yellow yolk. Vegie-rich Egg Meffins (savoury muffins; page 125) make a filling low-cal start.

BERRIES

Berries are your top fruit pick, as they're the highest in antioxidants and micronutrients, and very low in fructose, which can contribute to high blood sugar and insulin resistance (see page 15). Eat a range of colours, from blueberries through to raspberries and blackberries, in order to reap the range of antioxidant benefits. Always buy organic or chemical-free, as conventionally grown berries are treated with nasty sprays. Try my Layered Blueberry Pistachio Parfait (page 138).

ZUCCHINI

A member of the squash family, the zucchini (courgette) is a simple low-calorie vegetable rich in alkalising sodium that will restore your body to balance and rejuvenate the liver. It's lovely when grated into salads, made into grain-free zoodles (zucchini noodles), or sautéed or lightly steamed and finished with a squeeze of lemon and sea salt. You'll be surprised how filling you find just one slice of my Easy Zucchini Bread (page 136).

SEAWEED

Sea vegetables are incredibly rich sources of protein; vitamins A, B, C and E; trace elements; and minerals including zinc, calcium, iron and iodine. Dulse flakes are a great way to pack in a lot of nutrition by adding to bone broths or soups, or sprinkling like salt. Nori can be used to roll fish and vegetables, while wakame, arame and kombu can be added to soups or stews and to lentils and beans to improve digestibility. Get stuck into Vegie Nori Wraps (page 250).

FIVE FASTING SMART SWAPS

1

Replace pastry-bound quiches or flans with herb-filled omelettes or frittatas. You still get the flavour punch, but without the unnecessary carb-loaded pastry.

2

Replace watermelon and other high-fructose fruit with fresh or frozen berries for less of a sugar hit.

3

Replace regular pasta with vegetable pasta. Use zucchini (courgettes) to make zoodles or cucumber to make coodles, then steam or serve raw. Make thin ribbons using a spiraliser, vegetable peeler or mandoline.

4

Replace rice with cauliflower 'rice' – just grate cauliflower and steam or pan-fry with lemon or lime juice. Add some turmeric for colour.

5

Replace bread and wraps with vegie wraps, such as lettuce leaves, steamed bok choy (pak choy) or cabbage, and seaweed.

WEIGHT LOSS AND INFLUENTIAL FOODS

If losing weight is the main goal of your intermittent fasting protocol, then along with weight reduction through limiting your calories on your fasting days, you could try eating a range of these influential foods with powerful fat-burning and detoxification properties. With fat-burning foods, you can take a few different approaches.

Firstly, you can try foods that increase thermogenesis in the body. Thermogenesis is the process by which the body burns the foods you consume and converts them into heat. Secondly, you can consume foods high in antioxidant and detoxifying properties that will bind to toxins in the body, which can cause inflammatory weight gain, and remove them via the bowel. High-fibre foods will also help this process along, with the added benefit of helping you feel fuller for longer and taking longer to chew, which gives your brain time to register that you've had enough to eat. That's why it really does make sense to eat more fibre-rich vegetables.

Lastly, you can consume foods that enhance your gut ecology. Did you know that the bacteria each of us carry around in our gut outnumber our own human cells ten to one? It's therefore vitally important to take care of the good guys and keep them in balance so they can prevent obesity, metabolic disease, low-grade inflammation, raging appetite, slow metabolism, insulin resistance and other problems that have been scientifically linked to a gut overrun by strains of 'bad' bacteria.

While allowing your body to achieve a fat-burning state during periods of fasting, eating these foods throughout the week will add some extra fuel to the fire, burning even more calories and giving you an extra hand at shedding excess weight.

COCONUT OIL

This wonder hormone-balancing oil steadies your blood-sugar levels, is highly satiating due to its high saturated-fat content, and contains medium-chain fatty acids that have been shown to inhibit fat deposition through increased thermogenesis. Its mood-elevating capabilities will motivate you to exercise more, and it can ramp up your fat-burning potential. A study of obese men showed that ingesting 30 grams (1 ounce) of coconut oil each day for four weeks reduced waist circumference by 2.86 cm (1⅛ inches). Goodbye, stubborn belly fat! Add a tablespoon of coconut oil to smoothies and drinks on your non-fasting days and use it in moderation to replace other oils when cooking at high temperatures.

SUSTAINABLE SALMON

Salmon is high in omega-3 fatty acids, which help reduce levels of the hormone leptin (see page 15). As we have seen, leptin plays a critical role in controlling energy intake and energy expenditure, and lower leptin levels are linked with a faster metabolism. Replacing fatty red meats with salmon provides good fats that promote heart health. On fasting days, steam salmon or poach it in a small amount of coconut water, then add herbs, garlic, spices and lemon juice for calorie-free flavour. Add a little splosh of wheat-free tamari for a tangy Asian influence, and pair it with asparagus. Salmon sashimi with seaweed salad can be a great dish to order when eating out on fasting days, or try my Rocket and Salmon Midweek Omelette (page 215). On non-fasting days, scatter smoked salmon on cauliflower pizza bases (there's a recipe on superchargedfood.com) or roll it up in brown-rice sushi rolls.

CHILLI

Chillies, chilli flakes and cayenne pepper contain a fat-burning compound called capsaicin, which helps fight weight gain by increasing the metabolic rate, shrinking fat tissue, inhibiting fat accumulation and lowering lipid levels in the blood. For midweek eating, make up a batch of chilli con carne or a vegetarian hotpot, or add chilli to stir-fries. Pack your fasting-day menu with flavour by adding chilli to soups, steamed vegetables and eggs. It ramps up the metabolism-boosting powers of the Avo Cargoes on page 242.

WALNUTS

A randomised, double-blind crossover study of walnut consumption was conducted by the Harvard Medical School on 20 men and women with metabolic syndrome (i.e. increased blood pressure, high blood-sugar levels, excess body fat around the waist and abnormal cholesterol levels). The findings indicated that walnuts promote satiety and decrease appetite, and are therefore great for preventing overeating. Use this top nut as a healthy snack or as a crust for fish or chicken, add them to your curries and baked goods, and throw a handful into your salads for sweetness and crunch.

CINNAMON

This sweet spice is an excellent source of manganese, an important activator of the enzymes involved in healthy carbohydrate and fat metabolism. It's also a stabiliser of blood-sugar levels, preventing the kinds of sugar crashes that might lead you to reach for sweet foods to improve your overall mood. Adding half a teaspoon of ground cinnamon to herbal tea can aid weight loss, indigestion and bloating, and can satisfy cravings for sweet foods. Sprinkle it on your morning toast, or see how it adds a spark to my basic Jam-jar Porridge recipe (page 118). A perfect partner for cinnamon is apple or peach – you'll love my Baked Apple with Prune, Cinnamon and Cardamom (page 143).

BROCCOLI

These gorgeously green tree-like florets of goodness are skyscraper high in calcium, a known weight-reducer. They're also high in fibre and chlorophyll, which will sweep out toxic build-up from your digestive system. And they contain the detoxifying vitamins A, C and K. Whip up a green soup, grate broccoli onto salads, use it as a dipper, add it to your stir-fries, quiches and mash, or steam it with garlic and lemon for fasting days. Flip over to my Dressed Green Bean and Broccoli Salad (page 168).

GREEN TEA

This beverage has thermogenic qualities far exceeding those that can be explained by its caffeine content alone. Green tea has been proven to raise metabolic rates, speeding up fat burning, and has wonderful antioxidant benefits for the digestive tract. Use it as a poaching aid and whip up the Green-tea-poached Ginger Chicken (page 161). Or you could drink it in the morning or use it to make a healthy ice cream for non-fasting days by blitzing it up with coconut milk and a frozen banana in a food processor.

GINGER

This warming spice is highly anti-inflammatory, reduces blood pressure and promotes a healthy insulin response (see page 15). It has a stimulatory effect on the gastrointestinal tract, and has also been shown to enhance thermogenesis and reduce feelings of hunger. Regularly sipping hot water with a few slices of fresh ginger in it is a great way to keep your metabolism burning throughout the day. Use sliced ginger as a flavour aid when poaching and steaming on fasting days; make home-made ginger ale with grated ginger, mineral water and stevia; or eat it straight up – not for the faint-hearted! You'll love my Mint and Ginger Prawns with Coleslaw (page 205).

SUPERCHARGED TIP:
HOW TO AVOID
GARLIC BREATH

Got a hot date lined up? Chew
on some caraway or fennel seeds,
a sprig of parsley, mint leaves or
citrus peel for a couple of minutes
to neutralise garlic's noxious effect
and have significantly better breath.

GARLIC

This staple household ingredient has a powerful anti-obesity effect. Studies on overweight mice show that garlic reduces body weight and also lowers fat levels in the blood and liver. And it's a wonderful thermogenic ingredient to add some extra fat-burning fire to your body. Use this fat-flusher cooked or raw for benefits, and as a flavour booster in salads, marinades and sauces, even as a gentle spice rub. Try the Garlicky Vegie Pasta on page 224.

Pass on processed garlic salts and powder or the tubes of minced garlic you find in supermarkets. Any health benefits these once contained are long gone.

EXTRA VIRGIN OLIVE OIL

This lovely green oil is high in skin-moisturising and cholesterol-lowering monounsaturated fats, and also contains a unique phenolic compound known as oleuropein, which is proven to enhance thermogenesis. Be sure to use extra virgin olive oil only at very low-to-medium heats, or as a cold pouring oil – it's best used on salads. When cooked at high temperatures the oil becomes unstable, which will reduce the health benefits and can contribute to inflammatory weight gain. For cooking at high temperatures, use coconut oil instead.

FERMENTED FOODS

Sauerkraut, kimchi, kefir, yoghurt with live cultures and kombucha are all wonderful sources of probiotic bacteria to recolonise your gut and prevent the weight gain associated with a bad balance of bacteria. If you're new to fermented foods, start with very small amounts and work your way up as your body adjusts. Eating a tablespoon of cultured vegetables with meals, or taking sips of fermented beverages before or after a meal is the best way to gain benefits.

SWEET POTATO

Sweet potato, yams and taro contain unique fermentable fibres that have a prebiotic effect in the gut, feeding and promoting the growth of good bacteria. Consuming these on regular days will help you maintain a healthy gut ecology and ward off weight-increasing bad bacteria. Make a sweet potato hash, a classic casserole, or crinkle-cut chips baked with coconut oil and rosemary in the oven. Whiz up a soup with curry spices, ginger and garlic, or try a Stuffed Sweet Potato (page 254).

FIVE WAYS TO SUPERCHARGE YOUR FASTING DAY

Boost your mood with tension-taming magnesium – from foods such as pepitas (pumpkin seeds) and squash seeds, mackerel, avocados and bananas.

Add apple cider vinegar to drinks or meals to aid digestion.

Go wild with flavoursome herbs – many have medicinal qualities and all are low in calories.

Drink peppermint tea – it's a foolproof hunger-pang distractor.

Eat protein with every meal to keep you sated.

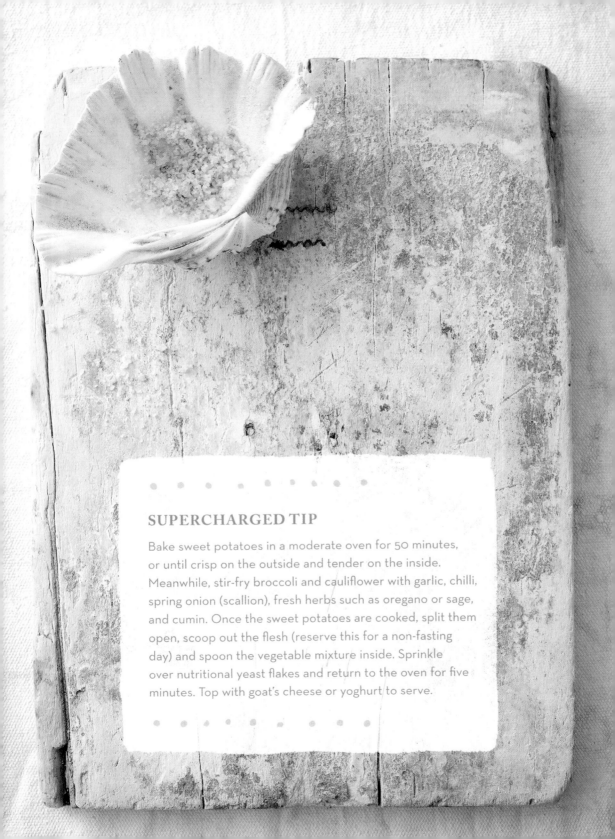

SUPERCHARGED TIP

Bake sweet potatoes in a moderate oven for 50 minutes, or until crisp on the outside and tender on the inside. Meanwhile, stir-fry broccoli and cauliflower with garlic, chilli, spring onion (scallion), fresh herbs such as oregano or sage, and cumin. Once the sweet potatoes are cooked, split them open, scoop out the flesh (reserve this for a non-fasting day) and spoon the vegetable mixture inside. Sprinkle over nutritional yeast flakes and return to the oven for five minutes. Top with goat's cheese or yoghurt to serve.

INGREDIENT CALORIE GUIDE

All figures given are calorie counts
per 100 grams (3½ oz) of the ingredients
in their uncooked state, unless otherwise
stated. The second, larger number in each
case is the same measure converted
to kilojoules (kJ).

CRUNCHABLE SALAD VEGETABLES *per 100 grams*

	Cal	kJ		Cal	kJ
Alfalfa sprouts	23	96	Cucumber	16	67
			1 medium	47	197
Avocado	160	670	Fennel	31	130
1 small	200	837	1 large bulb	73	306
Baby cos (romaine)					
lettuce, 1 whole	5	21	Kale	49	205
Bean sprouts	30	126	Lettuce	15	63
Cabbage	25	105	Radish, 1 medium	12	50
Capsicum (pepper),			Rocket (arugula)	25	105
1 medium	18	75	Snow peas		
yellow	27	113	(mangetout)	42	176
green	20	84	Snow pea		
red	31	130	(mangetout)		
Carrot	41	172	sprouts, 1 cup	35	147
1 small	21	88			
1 medium	25	105	Spinach,		
1 large	30	126	baby English	23	96
Celery	16	67	Tomatoes	18	75
1 medium stalk	6	25	1 medium	22	92
			Watercress	11	46

QUICK-STICK STEAMING VEGETABLES *per 100 grams*

	Cal	kJ		Cal	kJ
Asparagus	20	84	**Silverbeet**		
1 medium spear	15	63	**(Swiss chard)**	19	80
Artichoke, globe	47	197	**Spinach, English**	23	96
Baby corn	25	105	**Zucchini (courgette)**	17	71
Beans, green	31	130	1 small	20	84
Bok choy (pak choy)	13	54	1 medium	33	138
Broccoli	34	142	1 large	54	226
1 large head	136	569			
Cauliflower	25	105			
Edamame	122	511			
Leek	61	255			
1 medium (white part only)	40	167			
Peas	81	339			

ROASTING-PAN VEGETABLES *per 100 grams*

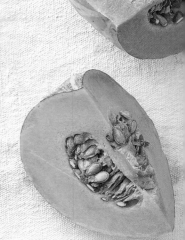

	Cal	kJ		Cal	kJ
Beetroot (beet)	43	180	Parsnip	75	314
Brussels sprouts	43	180	Pumpkin (winter squash)	26	109
Butternut pumpkin (squash)	45	188	Squash, baby (pattypan)	16	67
Daikon	18	75	Swede (rutabaga)	38	159
Eggplant (aubergine)	25	105	Sweet potato	86	360
1 small	110	461	Turnip	28	117

TURN-UP-THE-FLAVOUR INGREDIENTS *per 100 grams*

	Cal	kJ		Cal	kJ
Chilli	40	167	Mushrooms	22	92
1 small	12	50	Onion, 1 small	28	117
French shallot	72	301	1 medium	44	184
Garlic, 1 teaspoon	4	17	1 large	60	251
1 clove	5	21	Spring onion (scallion)	32	134
Ginger, 1 teaspoon, grated	2	8	1 medium	5	21
			Tomatoes, tinned	19	80

JUICY FRUITS *per 100 grams*

	Cal	kJ		Cal	kJ
Apple, 1 small	78	327	**Orange**, 1 small	45	188
1 medium	95	398	1 large	87	364
Apricot, 1 medium	17	71	**Orange juice**,		
Banana, 1 small	90	377	1 tablespoon	9	38
1 medium	105	440	**Peach**, 1 small	31	130
1 large	121	507	**Pear**, 1 small	85	356
Fig, 1 small	30	126	**Pineapple**,		
Kiwi fruit, 1 medium	42	176	1 cup (160 g/5½ oz)		
Lemon juice,			chunks	87	364
1 tablespoon	4	17	**Plum**, 1 medium	30	126
Lime juice,			**Pomegranate**,		
1 tablespoon	4	17	1 medium	233	976
Mango, 1 medium	200	837	**Prunes**, 1 medium	23	96
1 cup (185 g/6½ oz)			**Watermelon**, 1 cup		
diced	113	473	(175 g/6 oz) diced	49	205
Olive,	115	481			
1 small	4	17			

VITAMIN-C-PACKED BERRIES *per 100 grams*

	Cal	kJ
Açaí berries	70	293
Blackberries, 1 cup (130 g/4½ oz)	66	276
Blueberries, 1 cup (155 g/5½ oz)	90	377
Cranberries, 1 cup (95 g/3¼oz)	49	205
Goji berries, dried, 1 tablespoon	22	92
Grapes (botanically classified as a berry!)	62	260
Mixed berries, 1 cup (220 g/7¾ oz)	85	356
Raspberries, 1 cup (125 g/4½ oz)	69	289
Strawberries, 1 cup (150 g/5½ oz)	52	218

FLAVOUR-HIT HERBS AND SPICES

	Cal	kJ		Cal	kJ
Basil ¼ cup (7 g/¼ oz)	1.4	6	**Coriander**, ground, 1 tablespoon	20	84
Bay leaf, 1 medium	2	8	**Coriander (cilantro) leaves**, ¼ cup (7 g/¼ oz)	1	4
Capers, 1 tablespoon	3	13	**Cumin**, ground, 1 tablespoon	32	134
Cardamom, ground, 1 tablespoon	24	100	**Curry powder**, 1 tablespoon	6	25
Cayenne pepper, 1 teaspoon	6	25	**Dill**, 1 tablespoon	2	8
Chilli flakes, 1 teaspoon	6	25	**Dukkah**, 1 tablespoon	52	218
Chilli powder 1 teaspoon	8	33	**Fennel seeds** 1 tablespoon	7	29
Chives, chopped, 1 tablespoon	1.5	6	**Ginger**, ground, 1 tablespoon	6	25
Cinnamon, ground, 1 teaspoon	6	25	**Lemongrass**, 1 tablespoon	7	29
			1 stem	4	17

	Cal	kJ		Cal	kJ
Mint, 1 tablespoon	3.5	15	Sage, chopped, 1 tablespoon	8	33
Mustard powder, 1 teaspoon	16	67	Thyme, 1 tablespoon	4	17
Mustard, sugar-free, 1 teaspoon	3	13	Turmeric, ground and root 1 teaspoon	8	33
Nutmeg, grated, 1 teaspoon	11	46			
Oregano, chopped, 1 tablespoon	6	25			
Paprika, 1 teaspoon	6	25			
Parsley, chopped, 1 tablespoon	2	8			
Rosemary, picked, 1 tablespoon	3	13			

POWER-ON PROTEINS *per 100 grams*

	Cal	kJ
Beef, lean fillet	158	662
Beef, lean fillet steak	178	745
Beef, lean minced (ground)	212	888
Beef, lean stewing	203	850
Chicken breast, skinless	110	461
Chicken thigh, skinless	177	741
Lamb, lean minced (ground)	302	1264
Prawns	100	419
Salmon, smoked	117	490

Salmon, tinned	147	615
Sardines, in springwater	160	670
Scallops	111	465
Tuna, tinned	113	473
White fish (e.g. barramundi)	92	385

DIGESTIBLE DAIRY AND EGGS

	Cal	kJ		Cal	kJ
Cow's cheese, full-fat, 1 slice (28 g/1 oz)	113	473	Goat's cheese, 1 tablespoon	27	113
Egg, 1 medium (44 g/1½ oz)	63	264	Parmesan cheese, grated, 1 tablespoon	29	121
1 large (50 g/1¾ oz)	78	327	Sheep's cheese, 1 tablespoon	27	113
Egg white, 1 medium	15	63	Sheep's milk, yoghurt, 100 g (3½ oz)	104	435
			Yoghurt, plain, organic, no additives ½ cup (130 g/4½ oz)	79	331

GOOD FATS AND OILS

	Cal	kJ
Butter, organic, 1 tablespoon	136	569
Coconut oil, extra virgin, 1 teaspoon	39	163
Flaxseed oil, 1 teaspoon	40	167
Ghee, 1 tablespoon	149	624
Olive oil, cold-pressed extra virgin, 1 teaspoon	40	167
Sesame oil, 1 teaspoon	40	167

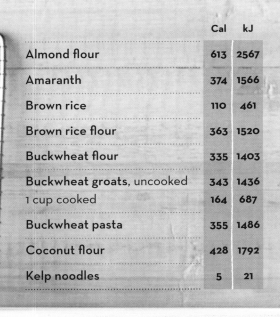

	Cal	kJ
Almond flour	613	2567
Amaranth	374	1566
Brown rice	110	461
Brown rice flour	363	1520
Buckwheat flour	335	1403
Buckwheat groats, uncooked	343	1436
1 cup cooked	164	687
Buckwheat pasta	355	1486
Coconut flour	428	1792
Kelp noodles	5	21

PANTRY-FILLING FLOURS, GRAINS AND SEEDS

per 100 grams

	Cal	kJ
Millet	378	1583
Nori, 1 sheet	9	38
Oats, gluten-free rolled	330	1382
Quinoa, uncooked	374	1566
1 cup	748	3132
Quinoa flakes	380	1591
Tapioca flour	357	1495
White rice	129	540

SIFT, SPRINKLE, SHAKE AND BAKE *per 100 grams*

	Cal	kJ		Cal	kJ
Baking powder, gluten- and additive-free, 1 teaspoon	2	8	Golden flaxmeal	534	2236
			Lemon zest, 1 teaspoon	1	4
Bicarbonate of soda (baking soda)	0	0	Lime zest, 1 teaspoon	1	4
Brown rice puffs	383	1604	Orange zest, 1 teaspoon	2	8
Cacao butter, 1 tablespoon	160	670	Plain (all-purpose) and self-raising flour, gluten-free	352	1474
Cacao nibs, 1 tablespoon	15	63	Vanilla extract, alcohol-free 1 teaspoon	12	50
Cacao powder, unsweetened, 1 tablespoon	24	100			
Coconut flakes	667	2793			

PULSATING PEAS AND BEANS
(COOKED/BOILED) *per 100 grams*

	Cal	kJ
Black-eyed peas	130	544
Cannellini beans	140	586
Chickpeas	164	687
Haricot beans	140	586
Lentils, brown	116	486
Pinto beans	22	92
Red kidney beans	127	532
Split peas	118	494

	Cal	kJ
Almond, 1 nut	7	29
Almonds, slivered, 1 tablespoon	63	264
Brazil nut, 1 nut	33	138
Cashews, 100 g (3½ oz)	553	2315
Chia seeds, 1 tablespoon	93	389
Flaxseed, 1 tablespoon	82	343
1 tablespoon ground	52	218
Hazelnut, 1 nut	9	38
Macadamia nut, 1 nut	19	80
Nut butter, 1 tablespoon	125	523
Pecan, 1 nut	20	84
Pepitas (pumpkin seeds), ¼ cup (40 g/1½ oz)	178	745
Pine nuts, 10 nuts	11	46
Sesame seeds, 1 tablespoon	69	289
Sunflower seeds, 1 tablespoon	78	327
Tahini, 1 tablespoon	119	498
Walnut, 1 nut	26	109

SAUCY CONDIMENTS AND SWEETENERS

	Cal	kJ
Apple cider vinegar, 1 tablespoon	4	17
Balsamic vinegar, 1 tablespoon	20	84
Beef stock, 1 cup (250 ml/9 fl oz)	30	126
Black pepper, freshly ground, ½ teaspoon	3	13
Celtic sea salt, ¼ teaspoon	0	0
Chicken stock, 1 cup (250 ml/9 fl oz)	20	84
Coconut sugar, 1 teaspoon	15	63
Dijon mustard, 1 teaspoon	3	13
Dulse flakes, 1 tablespoon	17	71
Fish stock, 1 cup (250 ml/9 fl oz)	13	54
Himalayan salt, ¼ teaspoon	0	0
Nutritional yeast flakes, 1 tablespoon	12	50
Rice malt (brown rice) syrup, 1 teaspoon	32	134
Stevia, 1 teaspoon	0	0
Tamari, wheat-free, 1 tablespoon	15	63
Tomato passata (puréed tomatoes), 100 ml (3½ fl oz)	30	126
Tomato paste (concentrated purée), 1 tablespoon	17	71
Vegetable stock/broth, sugar- and additive-free, 1 cup (250 ml/9 fl oz)	13	54
Xylitol, 1 teaspoon	10	42

NON-MOO MILKS *per 100 ml (3½ fl oz)*

	Cal	kJ
Almond and coconut milk	18	75
Almond milk	17	71
Cashew milk	72	301
Coconut cream	330	1382
1 tablespoon	65	272
Coconut milk	180	754
Oat milk	35	147
Rice milk	55	230

MEAL PLANS – WOMEN

WORKDAY FASTING MENU

	CALORIES	BREAKFAST	LUNCH	DINNER
DAY 1	495 calories (2073 kJ)	Minty Mango Smoothie (p114) 139 (582)	Vegie Soup in a Jar (p236) 90 (377) Thai Flavour Hit (p238) 48 (201)	Fish in a Creamy Mustard Sauce (p226) 218 (913)
DAY 2	490 calories (2051 kJ)	Basic Green Smoothie (p116) 96 (402)	Avo Cargo with tuna (p242) 259 (1084)	Aromatic Zucchini Curry (p196) 135 (565)
DAY 3	494 calories (2068 kJ)	Mexican Scrambled Eggs (p122) 180 (754)	Tomato-stuffed Zucchini Canoe with Avocado Tahini Dressing (p248) 103 (431)	Moroccan Quinoa Chicken (p202) 211 (883)
DAY 4	518 calories (2168 kJ)	Coconut Banana Bread (p134) 119 (498)	Egg-white Frittata with Silverbeet and Herbs (p247) 130 (544)	Steak with Caramelised Onions (p223) 269 (1126)
DAY 5	488 calories (2043 kJ)	Strawberry and Yoghurt Muffins (p126) 178 (745)	Vegie Nori Wrap (p250) 181 (758)	Curried Carrot Soup (p207) 129 (540)
DAY 6	501 calories (2098 kJ)	Cacao–Berry Smoothie (p112) 117 (490)	Tuna Lettuce Wrap (p179) 203 (850)	Smoked Salmon Living Lentil Bowl (p180) 181 (758)
DAY 7	554 calories (2319 kJ)	Choc Tahini Greenie (p112) 143 (599)	Green Bean, Radish and Avocado Salad (p166) 241 (1008)	Mexican Chicken and Avocado Salad (p211) 170 (712)

FASTING MENU FOR NON-WORKDAYS

	CALORIES	BREAKFAST	LUNCH	DINNER
DAY 1	499 calories (2089 kJ)	Baked Apple with Prune, Cinnamon and Cardamom (p143) 130 (544)	Ginger and Coriander Fish Fillet (p184) 158 (662)	Moroccan Quinoa Chicken (p202) 211 (883)
DAY 2	497 calories (2081 kJ)	Orange and Cinnamon Buckwheat Porridge (p119) 149 (624)	Goji Berry and Tomato Soup (p174) 149 (624)	Tamari Mushroom Beef Stir-fry (p201) 199 (833)
DAY 3	514 calories (2152 kJ)	Mustard and Chive Sweet Potato Hotcake (p128) 115 (481)	Smoked Salmon Living Lentil Bowl (p180) 181 (758)	Fish in a Creamy Mustard Sauce (p226) 218 (913)
DAY 4	496 calories (2077 kJ)	Zucchini and Coriander Egg Meffin (p123) 100 (419)	Chicken Meatballs with Marinara (p151) 178 (745)	Roasted Vegetable Quinoa (p225) 218 (913)
DAY 5	510 calories (2135 kJ)	Baked Apple Pancake (p130) 170 (712)	Asian Kelp Noodle Salad (p156) 161 (674)	Sautéed Scallops with Mushroom and Spinach (p194) 179 (749)
DAY 6	496 calories (2077 kJ)	Cacao-berry Smoothie (p112) 117 (490)	Red Onion and Zucchini Frittata (p188) 177 (741)	Garlicky Vegie Pasta (p224) 202 (846)
DAY 7	503 calories (2106 kJ)	Egg-white Omelette with Zucchini and Mushrooms (p160) 138 (578)	Stovetop Ratatouille (p190) 129 (540)	Asian Chicken Zoodles (p212) 236 (988)

MEAL PLANS – MEN

WORKDAY FASTING MENU

	CALORIES	BREAKFAST	LUNCH	DINNER
DAY 1	590 calories (2470 kJ)	Basic Green Smoothie (p116) 96 (402) Vegie-rich Egg Meffin (p125) 89 (372)	Tuna Lettuce Wrap (p179) 203 (850)	Garlicky Vegie Pasta (p224) 202 (846)
DAY 2	607 calories (2541 kJ)	Zucchini and Coriander Egg Meffin (p123) 100 (419)	Stuffed Sweet Potato (p254) 244 (1021)	Chicken and Cashew Stir-fry (p232) 263 (1101)
DAY 3	603 calories (2525 kJ)	Mexican Scrambled Eggs (p122) 180 (754)	Smoked Salmon Living Lentil Bowl (p180) 181 (758)	Baked Fish with Leeks and Fennel (p231) 242 (1013)
DAY 4	603 calories (2525 kJ)	Banana Pancakes with Blueberries (p129) 83 (348)	Bento Box (p252) 421 (1763)	Mediterranean Green Beans (p206) 99 (414)
DAY 5	589 calories (2465 kJ)	Spicy Baked Eggs (p120) 141 (590)	Lettuce Wraps with Lamb Mince (p255) 237 (992)	Moroccan Quinoa Chicken (p202) 211 (883)
DAY 6	593 calories (2483 kJ)	Coconut Banana Bread (p134) 119 (498)	Avo Cargo with chicken (p242) 256 (1072)	Fish in a Creamy Mustard Sauce (p226) 218 (913)
DAY 7	604 calories (2529 kJ)	Cafe-style Smoked Salmon, Eggs and Asparagus (p144) 160 (670)	Capsicum Cup (p245) 195 (816)	Scallop and Green Bean Curry (p218) 249 (1043)

FASTING MENU FOR NON-WORKDAYS

	CALORIES	BREAKFAST	LUNCH	DINNER
DAY 1	**601 calories (2516 kJ)**	Jam-jar Porridge (p118) 151 (632)	Smoked Salmon Living Lentil Bowl (p180) 181 (758)	Steak with Caramelised Onions (p223) 269 (1126)
DAY 2	**574 calories (2403 kJ)**	Choc Tahini Greenie (p112) 143 (599)	Lemon and Garlic Chicken Skewer (p172) 174 (728)	Rocket and Salmon Midweek Omelette (p215) 257 (1076)
DAY 3	**605 calories (2533 kJ)**	Mexican Scrambled Eggs (p122) 180 (754)	Pea, Fennel and Orange Soup (p171) 226 (946)	Tamari Mushroom Beef Stir-Fry (p201) 199 (833)
DAY 4	**601 calories (2516 kJ)**	Minty Mango Smoothie (p114) 139 (582)	Stuffed Sweet Potato (p254) 244 (1021)	Fish in a Creamy Mustard Sauce (p226) 218 (913)
DAY 5	**609 calories (2551 kJ)**	Choc Tahini Greenie (p112) 143 (599)	Pumpkin Almond Bake (p154) 217 (909)	One-pan Roasted Fish and Vegetables (p198) 249 (1043)
DAY 6	**593 calories (2483 kJ)**	Spicy Baked Eggs (p120) 141 (590)	Tuna Lettuce Wrap (p179) 203 (850)	Scallop and Green Bean Curry (p218) 249 (1043)
DAY 7	**586 calories (2454 kJ)**	Baked Apple Pancake (p130) 170 (712)	Egg-white Omelette with Zucchini and Mushrooms (p160) 138 (578)	Smoked Paprika Meatball Soup in a Flask (p258) 278 (1164)

PART 2

FASTING RECIPES

A GUIDE TO THE RECIPES

You'll notice a little scale icon next to each recipe indicating how many calories there are per serve. This isn't a forbidden-food diet book, but all recipes are free of gluten, wheat, processed sugar and yeast, and many are dairy-free just in case you're personally avoiding those foods for health or other reasons. Many recipes include handy shopping, preparation and cooking tips.

BREAKFAST

cacao–berry smoothie

117

calories per
serve (490 kJ)

Serves 2

Who wouldn't want to wake up to a powerful combo of magnesium-rich chocolate and a hit of sweet antioxidants in the morning? This concoction contains everything you need to set your immune system up to thrive. And with the help of cacao's brain-stimulating properties, it will enhance your mood and attitude for the day.

150 g (5½ oz/1 cup) blueberries
150 g (5½ oz/1¼ cups) raspberries
200 ml (7 fl oz) almond milk
1 tablespoon cacao powder
stevia, to taste (optional)

Combine all the ingredients in a blender and whiz until smooth.

choc tahini greenie

143

calories per
serve (599 kJ)

Serves 1

½ peeled and frozen banana
45 g (1½ oz/1 cup) baby English spinach leaves
  (or frozen English spinach)
1 teaspoon tahini
1 tablespoon raw cacao nibs
250 ml (9 fl oz/1 cup) almond milk
handful of ice (optional)

Combine all the ingredients in a blender and whiz until smooth.
Drink immediately.

Cacao–berry
Smoothie (left)
and Choc Tahini
Greenie (right)

minty mango smoothie

139

calories per serve (582 kJ)

Serves 2

Mint is a known appetite-suppressant, so pair it with the tropical sweetness of mango and you'll definitely be well set for satisfaction. If you need some extra filling, add a teaspoon (39 calories/163 kilojoules) of coconut oil to the mix for two people.

1 medium mango
handful of mint leaves
375 ml (13 fl oz/1½ cups) almond milk
1 tablespoon lime juice
stevia, to taste
ice cubes, to taste

Combine all the ingredients in a blender and whiz until smooth.

Fruity Breakfast
Smoothie (left), Basic
Green Smoothie (top
right) and Minty Mango
Smoothie (bottom right)

basic green smoothie

Serves 2

Evergreen green smoothies are high in phytonutrients and chlorophyll, and dense in plant minerals. This concoction also includes some fat-burning, anti-inflammatory ginger to aid weight loss.

250 ml (9 fl oz/1 cup) almond milk
2 handfuls of baby English spinach leaves
1 peeled and frozen small banana, in chunks
1 Lebanese (short) cucumber, roughly chopped
1 teaspoon grated ginger
stevia, to taste
ice cubes, to taste

Combine all the ingredients in a blender and whiz until smooth.

fruity breakfast smoothie

Serves 2

½ peeled and frozen banana
35 g (1¼ oz/¼ cup) mixed frozen berries
1 small peach, stone removed, chopped
500 ml (17 fl oz/2 cups) almond milk
10 g (¼ oz/¼ cup) quinoa flakes or 25 g (1 oz/¼ cup)
 instant gluten-free oats
½ teaspoon chia seeds

Combine all the ingredients in a blender and whiz until smooth.

SUPERCHARGED TIP

Freezing fruit is a brilliant way to ensure you always have
smoothie ingredients on hand, and is an economical habit too.
If you ever see fresh produce at a ridiculously low price, don't
wait until next week. Buy up big and store it in the freezer.
Frozen fruit can also be combined with smaller amounts of
liquid to make a delectable ice-cream substitute.

jam-jar porridge

151

_calories per
serve (632 kJ)_

Serves 1

35 g (1¼ oz/⅓ cup) gluten- and wheat-free rolled oats,
  soaked overnight (see tip)
¼ teaspoon Celtic sea salt
small pinch each of ground cinnamon and nutmeg
170 ml (5½ fl oz/⅔ cup) filtered water
60 ml (2 fl oz/¼ cup) almond milk
½ teaspoon alcohol-free vanilla extract
30 g (1 oz/¼ cup) raspberries
stevia, to taste (optional)

Combine the oats, salt, spices and water in a small saucepan over medium-high heat and bring to the boil. Reduce the heat to low and simmer for 8–10 minutes, until the mixture reaches the desired consistency. Spoon into a jam jar.

Combine the almond milk and vanilla extract, then pour over the porridge. Top with the raspberries and stevia (if using) to serve.

SUPERCHARGED TIP

Oats are most easily digested after an overnight soak in warm filtered water and 1 teaspoon lemon juice, or plain yoghurt with live cultures, or whey (the white liquid on top of yoghurt, which can also be strained from yoghurt through cheesecloth/muslin and used to soak other grains and pulses). Strain the oats in the morning. This preparation will ensure that your body can absorb the maximum amount of minerals from the oats.

orange and cinnamon buckwheat porridge

149

calories per serve (624 kJ)

Serves 1

Try this extra-cosy porridge on a cooler morning, especially if you're feeling a little blue. High-fibre buckwheat contains compounds that help ward off depression, while cinnamon stabilises blood sugar, sustaining your moods and appetite.

65 g (2¼ oz/⅓ cup) buckwheat groats
1 cinnamon stick
250 ml (9 fl oz/1 cup) filtered water, plus extra as needed
½ teaspoon ground cinnamon
½ teaspoon ground nutmeg
stevia, to taste
½ teaspoon alcohol-free vanilla extract
1 large orange, peeled and cut into segments

Rinse the buckwheat in cold water, then combine in a small saucepan with the cinnamon stick and the water. Bring to the boil, stirring frequently. Reduce the heat to low, add the ground spices, stevia and vanilla, then simmer, covered, for 6 minutes, adding more water if necessary.

Add the orange and cook for 5–6 minutes, to reach the desired consistency.

SUPERCHARGED TIP

I highly recommend investing in an organised spice rack. The magic of flavour-making lies in a basic understanding of spice combinations, although you usually can't go wrong adding them randomly. Try cumin, turmeric, coriander, garam masala and paprika in savoury dishes; and vanilla, ginger, nutmeg, cardamom and cinnamon for sweeter recipes.

spicy baked eggs

Serves 2

If you're bored with poaching, boiling, frying and omelette-ing, this
is the egg recipe for you. Eggs are such a trusty and cheap staple,
it's a shame to limit them to predictable cooking methods. This
exotic baked-egg dish will take your egg adoration to the next level.

1 teaspoon extra virgin olive oil, or your oil of choice
200 g (7 oz) cherry tomatoes, halved
1 small red capsicum (pepper), diced
½ red onion, chopped
1 garlic clove, finely chopped
45 g (1½ oz/1 cup) baby English spinach leaves
1 teaspoon ground cumin
½ teaspoon ground coriander
½ teaspoon paprika
pinch of ground cinnamon
2 medium eggs
Celtic sea salt and freshly ground black pepper, to taste
coriander (cilantro) leaves, to serve

~~~~~~

Preheat the oven to 220°C (425°F).

Heat the oil in a medium, heavy-based saucepan over medium heat.

Add the tomatoes, capsicum, onion, garlic, spinach and spices, then cook
for 10 minutes, stirring occasionally (add a little water if necessary to
prevent sticking).

Spoon the mixture into a 750 ml (26 fl oz/3 cup) capacity ovenproof dish or
frying pan, make two dents in the top of the mixture with the bottom of a
spoon and crack an egg into each. Season with salt and pepper, then bake
for 12–15 minutes, until the yolks are cooked to your liking.

Remove from the oven and serve with coriander leaves scattered over.

mexican scrambled eggs

Serves 2

Your cravings for Mexican food will be bottom-kicked with this colourful morning meal. The spicy addition of chilli powder will also kick-start thermogenesis within your body (see page 78), helping you burn more calories.

½ red capsicum (pepper)
½ green capsicum (pepper)
1 teaspoon olive oil
1 red onion, chopped
1 garlic clove, finely chopped
200 g (7 oz) tomatoes, chopped
½ teaspoon chilli powder or flakes, or ½ fresh red chilli

2 medium eggs
Celtic sea salt and freshly ground black pepper, to taste
50 g (1¾ oz/about ½ small) avocado, cut into dice
a few coriander (cilantro) leaves, to serve
squeeze of lime juice

Preheat the grill (broiler) to medium–high and line a baking tray with baking paper.

Place the capsicum halves (seeds removed first) onto the prepared baking tray and grill for 10 minutes, turning occasionally, until their skins have blistered and blackened. Transfer to a bowl, cover with plastic wrap and let cool for 15 minutes. Remove the skins and cut the capsicums into strips.

Heat the oil in a medium frying pan over medium heat, then add the onion, garlic, tomatoes, capsicum and chilli (finely chopped, if fresh). Cook for 15 minutes, or until the liquid has evaporated. Keep warm.

Beat the eggs and season with salt and pepper. Heat a small non-stick frying pan over low heat, then add the eggs and stir until they're set.

Serve the eggs with the capsicum mixture, topped with avocado and coriander leaves. Squeeze lime over the avocado for extra zing.

zucchini and coriander egg meffins

100

calories per
serve (419 kJ)

Serves 3

Meffins – savoury muffins – make the perfect start to any day.

1 teaspoon extra virgin olive oil
½ red onion, sliced
1 small zucchini (courgette), cut into fine dice
3 medium eggs
½ teaspoon ground turmeric
150 ml (5 fl oz) almond milk
2 tablespoons chopped coriander (cilantro)
Celtic sea salt and freshly ground black pepper, to taste

Preheat the oven to 190°C (375°F) and line six 80 ml (2½ fl oz/⅓ cup) muffin holes with paper cases.

Heat the oil in a medium frying pan over medium heat. Add the onion and fry for 3–4 minutes, until golden brown. Add the zucchini and cook for a further 5 minutes.

In a medium bowl, whisk the eggs with the turmeric, almond milk and coriander, then stir in the zucchini and onion. Season with salt and pepper, then spoon the mixture into the prepared muffin cases.

Bake for 15–20 minutes, until firm to the touch.

SUPERCHARGED TIP

Herbs are very easy to grow in pots on your balcony or windowsill, giving you the freshest of aromatic ingredients.

vegie-rich egg meffins

Makes 6

Here's a fun way to up the vegie variety in your life. No one says
no to a meffin (savoury muffin), and these lovelies are bursting
with benefits from the vegetable kingdom. Enjoy them warmed
or chilled – they're also husband- and children-approved.

6 large eggs
70 g (2½ oz/½ cup) cherry tomatoes, halved
30 g (1 oz/½ cup) broccoli florets
80 g (2¾ oz/½ cup) chopped brown onion
45 g (1½ oz/½ cup) diced mushrooms
1 teaspoon dried oregano
1 teaspoon dried basil
Celtic sea salt and freshly ground black pepper, to taste

Preheat the oven to 180°C (350°F) and line six 80 ml (2½ fl oz/⅓ cup)
capacity muffin holes with paper cases.

In a large bowl, whisk the eggs, then add the remaining ingredients and
stir to combine. Pour the mixture into the prepared muffin cases.

Bake for 20 minutes, or until just set.

SUPERCHARGED TIP

On a non-fasting day, add pumpkin (winter squash) to the mix.
It brings a beautiful sweet taste and extra flavour. You can omit
the onion if you don't want post-breakfast onion breath.

strawberry and yoghurt muffins

Makes 6

These deliciously sweet and creamy muffins can be made on a non-fasting day then stored in the freezer. Whip one out on a fasting day and warm in the oven. It'll really fill you up – if you're on two meals a day you can eat it midmorning and it'll carry you through to an early dinner. You can replace the strawberries with blueberries if you prefer.

1 teaspoon gluten-free baking powder
½ teaspoon bicarbonate of soda (baking soda)
1 tablespoon finely grated lemon zest
1 teaspoon powdered stevia or 12 drops liquid stevia
65 g (2¼ oz/½ cup) coconut flour

4 medium eggs
90 g (3¼ oz/½ cup/about 4 medium–large) chopped strawberries
1 teaspoon alcohol-free vanilla extract
60 ml (2 fl oz/¼ cup) light olive oil
130 g (4½ oz/½ cup) full-fat plain yoghurt

Preheat the oven to 180°C (350°F) and line six 80 ml (2½ fl oz/⅓ cup) muffin holes with paper cases.

Combine the baking powder, bicarbonate of soda, lemon zest, stevia and flour in a bowl and mix well. In a separate bowl, whisk the eggs, then mix in the strawberries, vanilla, oil and yoghurt. Add the dry ingredients to the wet and mix well. Spoon about 60 ml (2 fl oz/¼ cup) of the batter into each paper case.

Bake for 17–20 minutes, until a skewer inserted in the centre of a muffin comes out clean. Cool in the tin on a wire rack.

mustard and chive sweet potato hotcakes

Makes 6

These savoury hotcakes are loaded with sweet potato, one of nature's unsurpassed sources of beta-carotene. They're also highly anti-inflammatory, and help regulate blood-sugar levels. Make them ahead of time and refrigerate, then reheat in the oven on a fasting day. On non-fasting days, reheat in a frying pan with coconut oil.

500 g (1 lb 2 oz) sweet potatoes, peeled and roughly chopped
2 medium eggs
75 ml (2½ fl oz) almond milk
1 tablespoon gluten-free plain (all-purpose) flour
1 teaspoon gluten-free baking powder
2 tablespoons sugar-free mustard

½ teaspoon mustard powder
½ teaspoon ground cumin
1 tablespoon chopped chives
Celtic sea salt and freshly ground black pepper, to taste
1 teaspoon extra virgin coconut oil, or coconut oil spray, for shallow-frying

Cook the sweet potato in boiling water for 15 minutes or until tender. Drain well, then mash.

In a large bowl, whisk the eggs, then mix in the almond milk, flour, baking powder, mustard, mustard powder, cumin and chives. Season with salt and pepper. Add the egg mixture to the sweet potato and mix thoroughly. Refrigerate for 30 minutes, to help the mixture hold together during cooking.

Heat the oil in a medium frying pan over medium heat, then drop heaped tablespoons of batter into the pan. Cook for 5 minutes, turning halfway, or until golden on both sides.

Repeat with the remaining batter.

banana pancakes
with blueberries

Makes 3

1 large banana
1 large egg
pinch of stevia
a few drops vegetable oil
80 g (2¾ oz/½ cup) blueberries

~~~~~~~~~~

Peel and mash the banana, then add the egg and stevia. Mix well.

Heat the oil in a medium non-stick frying pan. Pour 60 ml (2 fl oz/¼ cup) of the batter into the pan and scatter one-third of the blueberries on top. Cook for 5–6 minutes, until lightly browned, then turn over and cook for 1–2 minutes on the other side.

Repeat with the remaining mixture and blueberries.

SUPERCHARGED TIP

It's tempting to reach for bargain berries, but it pays to invest in organic and chemical-free, for good reason. Because of their size, berries that are farmed non-organically have some of the highest levels of industrial pesticides. These pose a risk to your health and can contribute to inflammatory weight gain.

baked apple pancake

Serves 4

2 medium apples, peeled, cored and sliced
stevia, to taste
1 teaspoon lemon juice
3 medium eggs
65 g (2¼ oz/½ cup) tapioca flour
1 tablespoon coconut milk
125 ml (4 fl oz/½ cup) almond milk
pinch of Celtic sea salt
1 teaspoon ground cinnamon
pinch of nutmeg

Preheat the oven to 200°C (400°F) and line a 21 x 9 cm (8¼ x 3½ in) loaf (bar) tin with baking paper.

In a medium bowl, mix three-quarters of the apple slices with the stevia and lemon juice.

In a separate medium bowl, whisk the eggs, then mix in the flour, coconut milk, almond milk, salt and apple mixture. Let the batter rest for 10 minutes, then pour into the prepared tin. Top with the remaining apple slices, then sprinkle with the cinnamon and nutmeg.

Bake for 20–25 minutes, until set. Leave to cool for 10 minutes, cut into portions and serve warm.

SUPERCHARGED TIP

Letting the batter rest for 10 minutes before using is a good exercise in patience and results in a smoother mix and even hydration. This works for both baked and pan-cooked pancakes.

minty zucchini fritters

103

calories per fritter (431 kJ)

Makes 8

405 g (14¼ oz/3 cups) grated zucchini (courgette)
2 tablespoons chopped chives, plus extra to serve
15 g (½ oz/¼ cup) chopped mint, plus extra to serve (optional)
½ teaspoon chilli flakes, plus extra to serve (optional)
¼ teaspoon paprika

finely grated zest of 1 lime
1 tablespoon lime juice
2 medium eggs, lightly whisked
155 g (5½ oz/1 cup) brown rice flour
1 teaspoon baking powder
Celtic sea salt and freshly ground black pepper, to taste
1 teaspoon extra virgin coconut oil, or coconut oil spray

Using your hands, squeeze any excess liquid from the zucchini then combine in a large bowl with the chives, mint, chilli, paprika, lime zest and juice, and eggs. Stir to mix well.

In a medium bowl, combine the flour, baking powder, salt and pepper. Add the dry ingredients to the wet ingredients and mix well.

Heat a few drops of coconut oil in a medium frying pan over medium heat, then drop heaped tablespoons of batter into the pan. Cook on each side for 3–5 minutes, until golden. Repeat with the remaining batter.

Top with extra chives, mint and chilli flakes (if using), then serve.

SUPERCHARGED TIP

Many baking powders are laden with aluminium in the form of sodium aluminium sulfate or sodium aluminium phosphate. Choose aluminium-free baking powder or make your own by combining one part bicarbonate of soda (baking soda) with two parts cream of tartar for an aluminium-free, starch-free version.

coconut banana bread

Makes 8 slices

Your standard pre-office banana-bread fix will be a long-lost
memory with this scrumptious upgrade. This recipe is gluten-free
and free of any of the laboratory-derived ingredients found in
many commercial banana breads. Make it on a non-fasting day
and take a slice to work with you when fasting for a deliciously
filling late breakfast.

3 ripe small bananas
3 medium eggs, lightly whisked
90 g (3¼ oz/¼ cup) rice malt (brown rice) syrup
stevia, to taste
a few drops alcohol-free vanilla extract
30 g (1 oz/¼ cup) coconut flour
¾ teaspoon bicarbonate of soda (baking soda)
½ teaspoon salt
fruit, to serve (optional, on non-fasting days)

Preheat the oven to 180°C (350°F) and grease a 21 x 9 cm (8¼ x 3½ in) loaf
(bar) tin.

Peel and mash the bananas in a medium bowl. Add the eggs, rice malt
syrup, stevia and vanilla, then mix well. Add the flour, bicarbonate of soda
and salt, then mix well. Pour the mixture into the prepared tin.

Bake for 50 minutes, or until a skewer inserted in the centre of the bread
comes out clean. Completely cool in the tin on a wire rack, then slice and
serve with fruit (if using).

easy zucchini bread

Makes 8 slices

110

*calories per
slice (461 kJ)*

1 medium zucchini
  (courgette), grated
4 medium eggs
2 small ripe bananas, peeled
  and mashed
65 g (2¼ oz/½ cup)
  coconut flour
1 tablespoon melted ghee
  or light olive oil

1 tablespoon ground cinnamon
½ teaspoon ground nutmeg
1 teaspoon alcohol-free
  vanilla extract
1 teaspoon bicarbonate of
  soda (baking soda)
½ teaspoon salt
stevia, to taste

Preheat the oven to 180°C (350°F) and grease a 21 x 9 cm (8¼ x 4¼ in) loaf
(bar) tin.

Using your hands, squeeze any excess liquid from the zucchini then
set aside.

In a large bowl, lightly whisk the eggs, then add the remaining ingredients
and stir to combine. Add the zucchini to the mixture and stir until the batter
is evenly mixed.

Spoon the batter into the prepared tin and bake for 35–45 minutes, until
a skewer inserted in the centre of the bread comes out clean.

SUPERCHARGED TIP

Save money by making your own ghee. Simmer a block of butter in
a small saucepan over a heat that produces a mild gurgle. The milk
solids will separate, and after 15–20 minutes the solids at the bottom
of the pan will start to brown. At this point, remove the pan from the
heat and cool. Strain the liquid through two layers of cheesecloth
(muslin) and voilà, you have your own home-made ghee!

chocolate banana soft serve

Serves 1

1 peeled and frozen medium banana, in big chunks
1 tablespoon cacao powder
a few drops alcohol-free vanilla extract
splash of almond milk
stevia, to taste
ground cinnamon, to serve

Combine all the ingredients, except the cinnamon, in a blender, then whiz until smooth. Serve with a sprinkle of cinnamon.

SUPERCHARGED TIP

If you ever catch a bargain on bananas, stock up and freeze them. Simply peel them, chop them into chunks and keep them in the freezer as the perfect addition to smoothies, or defrost them and add to baked goodies.

layered blueberry pistachio parfait

196

calories per
serve (821 kJ)

Serves 4

125 ml (4 fl oz/½ cup) coconut cream
1 tablespoon lime juice
stevia, to taste
2 tablespoons chia seeds
310 g (11 oz/2 cups) blueberries (see tips)
20 pistachio nut kernels (optional)
finely grated zest of ½ lime (optional)

In a medium bowl, mix together the coconut cream, lime juice and stevia. Add the chia seeds and stir to combine. Set aside for 15 minutes to thicken.

Take half the blueberries and distribute them evenly between four glasses. Distribute the coconut cream mixture evenly between the glasses. Add another layer of blueberries to each glass. Top each with five pistachio kernels and a pinch of lime zest (if using).

Serve at room temperature, or refrigerate for 30 minutes then serve chilled.

SUPERCHARGED TIPS

Make this ahead of time and refrigerate for 4 hours or overnight for the chia seeds to reach their full volume. On non-fasting days, top with coconut flakes for the elegance of a parfait.

Maintain your stock of citrus fruits – they will keep for up to 1 month, sliced and frozen then sealed in a plastic snaplock bag in the fridge.

For juicier blueberries, cook them with 2 tablespoons water in a small saucepan over low heat for 1–2 minutes, until they start to soften.

orange chocolatey pudding

290

calories per serve (1214 kJ)

Serves 1

Jaffas are so yesterday. For a delectable confectionery switch-up, try this creamy orange and chocolate pudding based on avocado, which is rich in vitamins C, E and K. Avos are also high in monounsaturated fats that will keep you satiated for hours – just remember not to go overboard on quantity.

125 g (4½ oz/about 1 small) avocado
2 tablespoons cacao powder
1 tablespoon fresh orange juice
1 tablespoon rice malt (brown rice) syrup
1 teaspoon finely grated orange zest, plus extra to serve (optional)
a few drops alcohol-free vanilla extract
pinch of Celtic sea salt
pinch of ground cinnamon
filtered water or almond milk, to serve (optional)
orange slices, to serve (optional)

Whiz all the ingredients except the water or almond milk in a blender until smooth and creamy. Add a little water or almond milk if needed for a good consistency. Spoon into a bowl and refrigerate for at least 1 hour until thick. Serve topped with orange slices and zest (if using).

baked apple with prune, cinnamon and cardamom

130

calories per
serve (544 kJ)

Serves 1

Give your everyday apple a makeover with this comforting cold-morning breakfast. Apples and prunes are also super-high in fibre, to keep your digestive system squeaky clean and free from toxic build-up.

1 small apple, cored but left whole
1–2 tablespoons filtered water
½ teaspoon ground cinnamon
¼ teaspoon ground cardamom
¼ teaspoon grated ginger
2 prunes, pitted and chopped
stevia, to taste (optional)

Preheat the oven to 180°C (350°F).

Put the apple in a small baking dish with the water. Combine the cinnamon, cardamom, ginger, prunes and stevia (if using) in a small bowl, then spoon into the centre of the apple.

Bake for 35–40 minutes, until soft. To test, pierce the apple with a sharp knife; it should slide through easily.

Note: *The apple can be cooked up to a day ahead. It can be eaten cold or warmed in the oven before eating.*

cafe-style smoked salmon, eggs and asparagus

160

calories per serve (670 kJ)

Serves 3

When you want to bring the fancy cafe breakfast into the comfort of your own home, here's your recipe. Protein-rich eggs, chlorophyll-filled greens and delicious smoked salmon brimming with omega-3s will provide a morning meal of stately standards.

3 medium eggs
150 g (5½ oz) asparagus,
  sliced on the diagonal
1 tablespoon dukkah
150 g (5½ oz) smoked salmon
100 g (3½ oz) baby rocket
  (arugula)
microherbs, to serve

DRESSING
1 tablespoon lime juice
1 teaspoon sugar-free mustard
1 tablespoon chopped chives
Celtic sea salt and freshly
  ground black pepper, to taste

Put the eggs in a saucepan and cover with cold water. Bring to a gentle boil over medium heat, then reduce the heat to low and simmer for 5 minutes. Drain and cover in iced water. Once cool, peel and cut in half crossways.

Meanwhile, cook the asparagus in a steamer over a saucepan of boiling water until just tender. Peel if the outer layer is tough.

Combine all the dressing ingredients and mix thoroughly.

Place the dukkah in a small bowl and dip the eggs in to partially coat.

Arrange the smoked salmon on a plate, then top with the rocket, asparagus and eggs. Drizzle with the dressing, grind over some pepper, scatter over microherbs and serve immediately.

LUNCH

sweet sicilian caponata

Serves 2

1 teaspoon extra virgin
  olive oil
350 g (12 oz) eggplant
  (aubergine), cut into dice
125 ml (4 fl oz/½ cup) filtered
  water, plus extra as needed
1 small zucchini (courgette),
  cut into chunks
1 celery stalk, chopped
½ large brown onion, cut
  into dice
1 large tomato, chopped

1 tablespoon capers, rinsed
  and drained
small handful of green olives,
  sliced
stevia, to taste
2 tablespoons apple cider
  vinegar
1 teaspoon dried thyme
handful of basil leaves
freshly ground black pepper,
  to taste

Heat the oil in a large frying pan over medium heat. Add the eggplant and cook for 8–10 minutes, until soft. Add the water, a little at a time, to prevent the eggplant sticking to the pan.

While the eggplant is cooking, put the zucchini, celery, onion and tomato in a saucepan with a large splash of filtered water. Cook for 10–15 minutes, until the zucchini is tender. Add the cooked eggplant with the capers, olives, stevia, apple cider vinegar and thyme, then cook for a further 5 minutes.

Serve topped with basil leaves and pepper.

SUPERCHARGED TIP

When shopping, scan the shelves for bargains on non-perishable, additive-free items such as apple cider vinegar, capers, olives, olive oils, sardines and other recipe basics.

chicken meatballs
with marinara

Serves 4

400 g (14 oz) minced
  (ground) chicken
1 brown onion, chopped
1 garlic clove, crushed
1 tablespoon tomato paste
  (concentrated purée)
1 tablespoon sugar-free
  mustard
1 teaspoon dried Italian herbs
Celtic sea salt and freshly
  ground black pepper,
  to taste
1 teaspoon extra virgin olive oil
chopped parsley, to serve

TOMATO SAUCE
1 medium brown onion,
  finely chopped
400 g (14 oz) tinned diced
  tomatoes
1 teaspoon dried Italian herbs
½ teaspoon chilli flakes
drizzle of balsamic vinegar
chopped parsley, to taste
stevia, to taste

Preheat the oven to 180°C (350°F).

Combine the chicken mince, onion, garlic, tomato paste, mustard, dried
herbs, salt and pepper in a large bowl and mix well. Using clean hands,
divide and roll the mixture into twelve meatballs. Refrigerate for at least
30 minutes.

Meanwhile, combine the tomato sauce ingredients in a medium saucepan
and cook, uncovered, over low heat for 20 minutes, or until thickened.
Pour into a medium ovenproof dish.

Heat the oil in a medium frying pan over medium heat, then cook the
meatballs for 5–6 minutes, turning to brown all over. Sit the meatballs on
top of the tomato sauce and bake for 30–40 minutes, until cooked through.

Serve topped with the chopped parsley.

simple saag chicken curry

Serves 4

Spinach has been smoothied way too much. The time has arrived to
return this superstar ingredient to its cooked form, gently softened,
so its many vitamins and minerals can be easily absorbed through
your digestive system. This curry will do just the trick.

1 teaspoon extra virgin
  olive oil
400 g (14 oz) skinless chicken
  breast fillets, cut into strips
1 brown onion, sliced
2 garlic cloves, finely chopped
400 g (14 oz) tinned diced
  tomatoes
250 g (9 oz) baby English
  spinach leaves
1 teaspoon grated ginger

1 teaspoon grated fresh
  turmeric or ground turmeric
1 teaspoon ground cumin
1 teaspoon chilli flakes
pinch of ground cinnamon
6 curry leaves
150 ml (5 fl oz) almond milk
2 tablespoons coconut flour
2 tablespoons chopped
  coriander (cilantro), to serve
  (optional)

Heat a few drops of the oil in a medium frying pan over high heat, add the
chicken, onion and garlic, then cook, stirring frequently, for 5 minutes. Add
the remaining ingredients except the coriander, stir well, then cover and
cook for 15 minutes, or until the chicken is cooked through.

Remove the lid and simmer for a further 2–3 minutes, to let the curry thicken.

Serve topped with the coriander (if using).

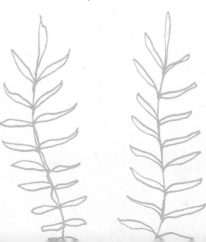

pumpkin almond bake

217

calories per serve (909 kJ)

Serves 4

A couple of everyday vegies combined with the right spices and a sprinkling of toasted almonds – you'll be amazed at the paradoxical simplicity and flavourful complexity of this dish. Easy to prepare and easy on the wallet, it's a bake that's big on flavour yet low in calories. What more could you ask? You can also replace the squash with zucchini (courgette).

600 g (1 lb 5 oz) pumpkin (winter squash), cut into large chunks
2 tablespoons extra virgin coconut oil, melted, or extra virgin olive oil
2 teaspoons fennel seeds
1 teaspoon ground cumin
½ teaspoon ground cinnamon

400 g (14 oz) baby (pattypan) squash, halved if large
1 large brown onion, cut into thin wedges
Celtic sea salt and freshly ground black pepper, to taste
45 g (1½ oz/⅓ cup) slivered almonds, to serve
soft herbs, to serve (optional)

Preheat the oven to 200°C (400°F).

Put the pumpkin in a roasting tin, drizzle with half the oil and sprinkle with the spices. Roast for 20 minutes, then add the remaining vegetables and oil, season with salt and pepper, and bake for a further 15–20 minutes, until cooked through, turning once.

Meanwhile, toast the slivered almonds in a small dry frying pan over medium heat until light golden.

Serve the vegetables topped with the toasted almonds and some herbs to garnish, if you like.

asian kelp noodle salad

Serves 3

340 g (12 oz) kelp noodles
150 g (5½ oz) bean sprouts, trimmed
3 medium spring onions (scallions), thinly sliced or curled
1 small carrot, cut into matchsticks or coarsely grated
1 medium Lebanese (short) cucumber, cut into matchsticks
½ large red capsicum (pepper), cut into thin strips

2 tablespoons chopped almonds
2 tablespoons coriander (cilantro) leaves
2 tablespoons mint leaves

DRESSING
1 tablespoon sesame oil
1 tablespoon wheat-free tamari
2 tablespoons lime juice
½ teaspoon chilli flakes
1 teaspoon grated ginger (optional)
stevia, to taste

Combine the dressing ingredients in a small bowl.

Rinse and drain the kelp noodles, then cut to the desired length. Put the noodles in a bowl, add the remaining ingredients and dressing, toss gently, then serve.

SUPERCHARGED TIP

Kelp noodles, a starch-free, gluten-free step up from regular refined rice, wheat or egg noodles, will fill you up without adding unnecessary calories. They're made from a brown seaweed that grows in deep waters and are high in calcium, iron and vitamin K, making them great for strengthening bones and increasing energy. You'll find them in Asian grocers and health food stores.

lemongrass chicken with grilled asparagus

227

calories per serve (950 kJ)

Serves 1

1 teaspoon finely chopped
  lemongrass stem
1 teaspoon finely grated
  lime zest
1 teaspoon lime juice
1 tablespoon lemon juice
2 garlic cloves, crushed
1½ teaspoons grated ginger
chilli flakes
140 g (5 oz) skinless chicken
  breast fillets

Celtic sea salt and freshly
  ground black pepper, to taste
½ teaspoon extra virgin
  coconut oil, melted
5 medium asparagus spears
½ teaspoon extra virgin
  olive oil
1 tablespoon chopped
  coriander (cilantro) or
  micro coriander, to serve
sliced fresh chilli (optional),
  to serve

Using a mortar and pestle, pound the lemongrass, lime zest and juice, lemon juice, garlic, ginger and chilli flakes until they form a thick paste. Rub the paste all over the chicken, then season with salt and pepper. Cover and refrigerate for 20 minutes.

Preheat the oven to 180°C (350°F).

Put the chicken on a small baking tray, drizzle with the coconut oil and bake for 25–30 minutes, until golden brown and cooked through.

While the chicken is cooking, preheat a chargrill pan or frying pan over medium heat. Add the asparagus and drizzle over the olive oil. Cook for 3–4 minutes, turning regularly – it will start to brown in spots.

Halve the asparagus, arrange it on a plate and place the chicken on top. Serve with coriander and chilli (if using) scattered over.

egg-white omelette with zucchini and mushrooms

138

calories per serve (578 kJ)

Serves 1

Egg-white omelettes are a great protein-rich fasting breakfast. You can pack in any sliced seasonal vegetables or herbs you have on hand to maximise the vitamin and mineral content, but this combination of earthy mushrooms and warming spices is a match made in heaven.

45 g (1½ oz/½ cup) mushrooms, sliced
1 small zucchini (courgette), thinly sliced
a few drops filtered water
4 medium egg whites, lightly whisked
1 teaspoon ground cumin
½ teaspoon ground coriander
Celtic sea salt and freshly ground black pepper, to taste
1 teaspoon extra virgin olive oil

~~~~~~~

Put the mushrooms in a small non-stick frying pan with the zucchini and water, then cook over high heat for 1 minute until lightly golden. Transfer to a medium bowl and allow to cool slightly.

Add the egg white and spices to the vegetable mixture, then stir to combine and season with salt and pepper.

Heat the oil in the same small frying pan over low heat then add the egg-white mixture. Cover and cook for about 5 minutes, until the egg is set.

Slide onto a waiting plate.

green-tea-poached ginger chicken

Serves 4

2 litres (70 fl oz/8 cups)
  filtered water
4 green tea bags
1 lemongrass stem, white
  part only
2.5 cm (1 in) piece of ginger,
  grated
1 tablespoon finely grated
  lime zest
3–4 mint leaves
560 g (1 lb 4½ oz/4 small),
  skinless chicken breast fillets
1 teaspoon ghee
4 garlic cloves, crushed

1 tablespoon lime juice, plus
  extra to serve
1 tablespoon apple cider vinegar
1 tablespoon wheat-free tamari
1 tablespoon almond butter
250 g (9 oz) green beans,
  trimmed and cut into 2.5 cm
  (1 in) lengths
12 cherry tomatoes, halved
Celtic sea salt and freshly
  ground black pepper, to taste
1 tablespoon sesame seeds,
  toasted in a dry frying pan

Pour the water into a medium saucepan then add the tea bags, lemongrass, ginger, lime zest and mint. Bring to the boil, then cover, turn off the heat and leave for 10 minutes to steep. Strain the tea, then return to the saucepan and bring to a simmer. Add the chicken breasts and simmer for 9–12 minutes until cooked through. Remove the chicken from the liquid, slice into long, thin pieces and set aside. Reserve the tea.

Meanwhile, melt the ghee in a medium frying pan over medium heat, then add the garlic and stir-fry for 1–2 minutes. Transfer to a small bowl, then add the lime juice, vinegar, tamari, almond butter and 170 ml (5½ fl oz/⅔ cup) of the reserved tea. Stir to combine.

Put the beans and tomatoes in the pan, then pour over the garlic tea mixture. Cook for 4–5 minutes, until the beans start to soften. Transfer the chicken to serving plates, season with salt, pepper and lime juice, then top with the beans and sauce. Sprinkle over the sesame seeds.

grilled lemon prawns
on cauli mash

Serves 1

Prawns are an excellent source of selenium, niacin, zinc, vitamin B12
and omega-3 fatty acids, making them a powerful energy-boosting,
inflammation-busting food. Enjoy them combined with this hearty,
starch-free cauliflower mash.

250 g (9 oz/about ½ small) cauliflower, cut into large florets
125 ml (4 fl oz/½ cup) chicken stock
1 tablespoon nutritional yeast flakes
75 g (2¾ oz/5 medium) peeled and deveined raw prawns (shrimp),
   tails left intact
finely grated zest of 1 lemon
1 teaspoon extra virgin olive oil
1 tablespoon chopped coriander (cilantro) or micro coriander,
   plus extra to serve (optional)
Celtic sea salt and freshly ground black pepper, to taste
lemon wedge, to serve (optional)

~~~~~~

Steam the cauliflower over a saucepan of boiling water, covered, for
12–15 minutes, until verging on soft but not falling apart. Transfer to a food
processor and blend, adding as much of the chicken stock as necessary
to make the texture smooth. Add the nutritional yeast and whiz again.

Meanwhile, combine the prawns with the remaining ingredients in
a medium bowl, then cover and set aside for 15 minutes.

Heat a medium frying pan over medium–high heat, then sauté the prawns
for 5–6 minutes, until cooked through.

Serve the prawns with the cauliflower mash, extra coriander and a lemon
wedge (if using).

mushroom, broccoli and sunflower seed quinoa pilaf

282

calories per serve (1181 kJ)

Serves 1

Mushrooms are a natural weight-loss food, providing maximum deliciousness with minimal calories. Their addictive flavour comes from an amino acid called glutamic acid, the same one found in monosodium glutamate (MSG), but mushrooms will satisfy your tastebuds without any unpleasant side effects.

1½ tablespoons uncooked quinoa

90 g (3¼ oz/1 cup) sliced button mushrooms

200 g (7 oz/about ½ large head) broccoli, cut into florets

¼ teaspoon ground cinnamon

½ teaspoon ground cumin

¼ teaspoon ground turmeric

125 ml (4 fl oz/½ cup) filtered water, plus extra as needed

Celtic sea salt and freshly ground black pepper, to taste

handful of mint leaves, roughly chopped

squeeze of lemon juice or lemon slices

1 tablespoon sunflower seeds

Rinse the quinoa in a fine-mesh sieve under cold water, then drain.

Heat a medium saucepan over medium heat, then add the mushrooms and broccoli with a little extra water and cook, stirring frequently, for 5 minutes. Add the cinnamon, cumin and turmeric, then reduce the heat to low and cook, stirring constantly, for 30 seconds, or until fragrant. Add the quinoa and cook, stirring constantly, for 2 minutes. Add the water, increase the heat to medium and bring to the boil, then cover, reduce the heat to low and cook for 12–15 minutes, until the quinoa is cooked through.

Season with salt and pepper.

Serve the pilaf topped with mint, with a squeeze of lemon or lemon slices and the sunflower seeds sprinkled over.

green bean, radish and avocado salad

Serves 1

Radishes, green beans and avocado make an aesthetically pleasing combination. It's always gorgeous to see the bright-pink hue of radishes with a contrast of greenery, and with every peppery, satisfying crunch they'll provide you with an impressive hit of vitamin C.

200 g (7 oz) green beans
60 g (2¼ oz/about ½ small) avocado, cut into large dice or sliced
5 medium radishes, sliced

APPLE CIDER VINAIGRETTE
2 tablespoons apple cider vinegar
1 teaspoon sugar-free mustard
½ teaspoon mustard powder (optional)
Celtic sea salt and freshly ground black pepper, to taste
stevia, to taste

Steam the green beans until just tender, then set aside to cool.

Combine all the vinaigrette ingredients and mix thoroughly.

Put the beans, avocado and radishes in a serving dish, then drizzle over the vinaigrette.

dressed green bean and broccoli salad

Serves 3

3 medium eggs
125 g (4½ oz) green beans
200 g (7 oz) broccoli florets
50 g (1¾ oz) baby English
   spinach leaves
40 g (1½ oz) black olives,
   pitted and sliced

DRESSING
1 tablespoon extra virgin
   olive oil
2 teaspoons apple cider
   vinegar
½ teaspoon chilli flakes
Celtic sea salt and freshly
   ground black pepper,
   to taste

Put the eggs in a small saucepan, cover with cold water and bring to the boil. Simmer for 5–10 minutes, depending on how runny you like the yolks (soft eggs make a nice contrast to the crunchy vegetables). Rinse under cold water, then peel and cut in half lengthways.

While the eggs are cooking, steam or blanch the green beans and broccoli, until just tender.

Make the dressing by combining all the ingredients.

Divide the spinach between three plates then top with the eggs, green beans and broccoli. Drizzle over the dressing and scatter over the olive slices.

SUPERCHARGED TIP

To ensure greens retain their highest nutrient status, wash, chop and seal them in a snaplock bag with all the air squeezed out. This prevents oxidisation and the loss of beneficial properties.

pea, fennel and orange soup

226

*calories per
serve (946 kJ)*

Serves 3

1 teaspoon extra virgin olive oil
1 medium brown onion, thinly sliced
1 garlic clove, finely chopped
500 g (1 lb 2 oz) fresh or frozen peas
1 large fennel bulb, trimmed and chopped
750 ml (26 fl oz/3 cups) vegetable stock or filtered water
finely grated zest and juice of 1 orange
2 tablespoons finely chopped parsley
2 tablespoons almond milk
Celtic sea salt and freshly ground black pepper, to taste
mint, to serve (optional)

Heat the oil in a large frying pan over medium heat, add the onion and garlic, then cook for 3–4 minutes, until softened. Add the peas, fennel, stock or water (add less liquid for thicker soup), orange zest and juice and parsley, then bring to the boil. Reduce the heat to low, return to a simmer and cook for 5–8 minutes, until the vegetables are tender. Add the almond milk.

Cool for a few minutes, then transfer to a blender, season with salt and pepper, and blend until smooth. (For a coarser texture reserve some of the cooked peas, roughly mash then add to the puréed soup.)

Serve topped with mint (if using) and pepper.

SUPERCHARGED TIP

Next time you're at the supermarket, remember that it always pays to have a packet or two of frozen peas in the freezer for a last-minute affordable addition to meals. Their gorgeous green hue adds a pop of sweet freshness to salads, pilafs and vegetarian dishes.

lemon and garlic chicken skewers

174

calories per serve (728 kJ)

Serves 4 (2 skewers per serve)

400 g (14 oz) skinless chicken
  breast fillets, cut into
  16 pieces
1 large zucchini (courgette),
  cut into 8 pieces
8 mushrooms, halved if large
1 small red capsicum (pepper),
  cut into 8 squares
1 small red onion, cut into
  8 pieces
1 teaspoon extra virgin
  olive oil

MARINADE
finely grated zest of 1 lemon
juice of 2 lemons
2 garlic cloves, finely chopped
1 teaspoon extra virgin
  olive oil
2 teaspoons dried oregano
1 tablespoon thyme leaves
Celtic sea salt and freshly
  ground black pepper,
  to taste

Combine the marinade ingredients in a large bowl and mix well. Mix in the chicken and vegetables, then cover and refrigerate for at least 1 hour.

Thread the chicken and vegetables onto eight pre-soaked bamboo skewers.

Heat a chargrill pan or frying pan over high heat, then drizzle with the oil. Cook the skewers for 7–8 minutes, turning occasionally, until the chicken is cooked through.

Serve immediately.

SUPERCHARGED TIP

I suggest whipping the marinade together and combining with the chicken first thing in the morning, to ensure deep permeation of the flavours into the chicken by lunchtime.

goji berry and tomato soup

Serves 4

100 g (3½ oz/1 cup) dried goji berries
filtered water, as needed
1 tablespoon extra virgin olive oil
1 large brown onion, cut into dice
2 garlic cloves, finely chopped
1 celery stalk, thinly sliced
1 small red chilli, finely chopped
200 g (7 oz/1 cup) chopped tomatoes
1 teaspoon cumin seeds, plus extra for serving (optional)
500 ml (17 fl oz/2 cups) vegetable stock
1 large handful of basil leaves
freshly ground black pepper, to taste
lemon oil, for drizzling (optional)

~~~~~~~~~

Rinse the goji berries in cold water and place in a bowl. Cover with filtered water and soak for a few minutes, then drain and set aside. (You could reserve the liquid and use it to replace some of the stock if you like.)

Heat the olive oil in a medium saucepan over medium heat. Add the onion, garlic, celery and chilli, then cook for 2–3 minutes. Add the tomatoes and goji berries, then the cumin seeds, reserving a few as a garnish. Stir for a further 2 minutes. Add the stock and bring to the boil, then reduce the heat to low and simmer for 10 minutes.

Allow to cool a little, then add the basil, reserving a little to use as a garnish, and blend until smooth using a hand-held blender or a food processor.

Serve topped with the reserved basil leaves and cumin seeds, a grind of black pepper and a drizzle of lemon oil (if using).

Optional: *Swirl in 1 teaspoon of full-fat plain yoghurt (3 calories/13 kJ).*

layered niçoise salad

197

*calories per
serve (825 kJ)*

Serves 4

400 g (14 oz) green beans, trimmed and halved lengthways
boiling water, to cover
2 baby cos (romaine) lettuce, leaves separated
200 g (7 oz) cherry tomatoes, halved
425 g (15 oz) tinned tuna in springwater, drained
2 medium hard-boiled eggs, peeled and halved or quartered lengthways

DRESSING
1 tablespoon apple cider vinegar
1 tablespoon lemon juice
1 teaspoon sugar-free mustard
Celtic sea salt and freshly ground black pepper, to taste

Place the green beans in a large bowl and cover with boiling water. Leave
for 2–3 minutes, then drain and rinse under cold water.

Layer the salad ingredients on a plate, starting with the lettuce leaves
as a base, then adding the beans, then the tomatoes, tuna and eggs.
(Alternatively, combine these components in a large bowl and toss gently.)

Combine the dressing ingredients and drizzle over the salad.

SUPERCHARGED TIP

For a quick protein hit in the middle
of a fasting slump, try a boiled egg.
I boil up several and keep them in the
fridge in their shells for up to 1 week.

tuna lettuce wraps

Serves 3

These tasty tuna wraps are a fun way to use up an affordable
tinned staple. Tuna is incredibly high in selenium, in the unusual
form selenoneine, an antioxidant that protects the fish's own
red blood cells from free-radical damage. We're likely to benefit
from these same free-radical-fighting properties when we eat
this remarkable fish.

1 small Lebanese (short) cucumber, cut into fine dice
1 celery stalk, cut into fine dice
1 small carrot, finely grated
3 spring onions (scallions), thinly sliced
½ teaspoon chilli flakes, or more to taste (or use a fresh red chilli)
1 teaspoon wheat-free tamari
1 tablespoon apple cider vinegar
stevia, to taste (optional)
425 g (15 oz) tinned tuna in springwater, drained
6 large iceberg lettuce leaves
6 cherry tomatoes, halved
roughly chopped mint and coriander (cilantro) leaves, to serve
squeeze of lime juice

~~~~~~~

In a medium bowl, combine the cucumber, celery, carrot, spring onions,
chilli, tamari, vinegar and stevia (if using).

Place three of the lettuce leaves inside another three to create three
double cups. Divide the tuna between the lettuce cups, then top with the
vegetable mixture and tomatoes.

Serve topped with the mint, coriander and lime juice.

smoked salmon living lentil bowl

Serves 2

1 teaspoon extra virgin olive
  oil
1 small brown onion, chopped
1 garlic clove, finely chopped
1 teaspoon grated ginger
50 g (1¾ oz) brown lentils,
  rinsed
375 ml (13 fl oz/1½ cups)
  chicken stock or filtered
  water
1 tablespoon ground cumin

1 handful coriander (cilantro),
  chopped
2 tablespoons capers, rinsed
100 g (3½ oz) baby English
  spinach leaves
100 g (3½ oz) smoked salmon
35 g (1¼ oz/½ cup) snow pea
  (mangetout) sprouts
freshly ground black pepper,
  to taste (optional)
squeeze of lemon juice

Heat the oil in a medium saucepan over medium heat. Add the onion, garlic and ginger, then cook for 3–4 minutes, until softened. Add the lentils, stock or water and cumin. Bring to the boil, then reduce the heat to low and simmer for 20–25 minutes, until the lentils are tender and the liquid has been absorbed. Stir through the coriander and capers.

Arrange all the ingredients in serving bowls, then season with a grind of pepper (if using) and finish with a squeeze of lemon juice.

SUPERCHARGED TIP

Lentils are a brilliant low-cost source of vegetarian protein. If you want to gain maximum nutritional value from lentils and make them more digestible, you can sprout them by placing them in a fine-mesh sieve or a sprouting jar and rinsing a few times a day for 2 days before you cook them. The lentils will grow little tails.

teacup watermelon salad

144

calories per
serve (603 kJ)

Serves 3

350 g (12 oz/2 cups) diced seedless watermelon
90 g (3¼ oz/2 cups) baby English spinach leaves
small handful of mint leaves, torn or roughly chopped
1 large celery stalk, thinly sliced
½ red onion, thinly sliced
60 g (2¼ oz/½ cup) crumbled goat's cheese

DRESSING
1 teaspoon lemon juice
1 teaspoon lime juice
handful of coriander (cilantro) leaves, chopped
130 g (4½ oz/½ cup) sheep's milk yoghurt
Celtic sea salt and freshly ground black pepper, to taste

~~~~~~

Whisk all the dressing ingredients together in a small bowl.

Combine the salad ingredients in a large bowl, then divide between three wide-mouthed teacups, mugs or bowls. Spoon the dressing on top and serve immediately.

SUPERCHARGED TIP

Keep the salad and dressing separate
until just before serving, then when
you're ready to eat spoon the
dressing on top.

ginger and coriander fish fillet

Serves 1

Fish is one of my favourite fasting ingredients, and there are so
many ways you can bring it to life. This Asian-inspired combination
of thermogenic ginger, detoxifying coriander, immune-boosting
garlic and metabolism-elevating coconut is a truly tantalising way
to dress up your seafood.

1 garlic clove, finely chopped
1 tablespoon finely chopped coriander (cilantro), plus extra to serve
1 teaspoon finely grated ginger
2 teaspoons coconut cream
125 g (4½ oz) white fish fillet (such as barramundi or cod)
1 tablespoon lime juice
rocket (arugula), to serve (optional)

~~~~~~

Preheat the oven to 200°C (400°F).

In a small bowl, combine the garlic, coriander and ginger. Add the coconut
cream and mix well.

Add the fish and the lime juice to the bowl with the garlic mixture, ensuring
the fish is well coated in marinade. Cover and refrigerate for 15 minutes.

Lay the fish on a 30 cm (12 in) square sheet of baking paper. Loosely seal
the fish in the parcel, then place on a baking tray and bake for 15 minutes
or until cooked through.

Serve topped with the extra coriander and rocket (if using).

Note: *This fish can also be cooked with a drop of oil in a frying pan on the
stovetop over medium–low heat if preferred.*

prawn, mango and avocado salad

301

calories per serve (1260 kJ)

Serves 2

150 g (5½ oz/10 medium) cooked, peeled and deveined prawns
  (shrimp), tails left intact
170 g (6 oz/about ½ medium) mango, cut into dice
60 g (2¼ oz/about ½ small) avocado, chopped
½ Lebanese (short) cucumber, chopped
100 g (3½ oz) rocket (arugula)
handful of bean sprouts, trimmed
1 spring onion (scallion), sliced or curled
mint leaves, to serve
coriander (cilantro) leaves, to serve (optional)

DRESSING
finely grated zest and juice of 1 lime
½ teaspoon chilli flakes
1 tablespoon extra virgin olive oil
stevia, to taste

Combine all the salad ingredients except the herbs in a serving bowl.

In a small bowl, combine all the dressing ingredients and mix well.

Drizzle the dressing over the salad, then serve topped with the mint
and coriander leaves (if using).

red onion and zucchini frittata

Serves 2

1 teaspoon extra virgin olive oil
1 small zucchini (courgette), cut into dice
1 garlic clove, finely chopped
½ red onion, sliced
70 g (2½ oz/½ cup) cherry tomatoes, halved
small handful of basil, torn
4 medium eggs
Celtic sea salt and freshly ground black pepper, to taste

Heat the oil in a small frying pan over medium heat. Add the zucchini, garlic and onion, then cook for 5–7 minutes, until the zucchini is tender. Add the tomatoes and basil, then increase the heat to medium–high and cook for about 5 minutes, until any moisture has evaporated.

Whisk the eggs in a large bowl, then season with salt and pepper. Add the zucchini mixture and stir to combine. Pour the mixture back into the pan and cook over medium heat until the eggs are set.

Note: *The frittata can be browned under the grill (broiler) at the end
if preferred.*

SUPERCHARGED TIP

Eggs can be a saviour on slow days. To get a complete meal on the table, you can make a frittata with just about any vegetables or herbs – thinly sliced, sautéed or roasted. Contrary to popular belief, eggs shouldn't be stored in the little holes on the fridge door, but for up to 6 weeks in the original carton in the main area of the fridge, where the temperatures are stable. The cartons also prevent water loss and protect the eggs from soaking up other flavours.

stovetop ratatouille

Serves 2

1 teaspoon extra virgin coconut oil or olive oil
1 large brown onion, sliced
1 small red capsicum (pepper), roughly chopped
1 orange capsicum (pepper), roughly chopped
1 large zucchini (courgette), roughly chopped
2 tomatoes, chopped
1 garlic clove, finely chopped
stevia, to taste (optional)
125 ml (4 fl oz/½ cup) vegetable stock or filtered water
1 teaspoon dried oregano
Celtic sea salt and freshly ground black pepper, to taste
handful of parsley or basil, chopped

Heat the oil in a large frying pan over medium heat, then add the onion and
cook for 3–4 minutes, until softened. Stir in the capsicums, zucchini, tomatoes,
garlic and stevia (if using). Add the stock or water and oregano, bring to the
boil, then reduce the heat to low and simmer, covered, for 30 minutes.

Season with salt and pepper. Add the parsley or basil, cook for another
2–3 minutes, then serve immediately or cool and refrigerate for later use.

SUPERCHARGED TIPS

Add a handful of baby English spinach leaves (6 calories/25 kJ) for
extra greenery.

Ratatouille is a freezer-friendly fasting dish. I suggest doubling or
even tripling many of the stew, soup or curry recipes in this book
so you're always stocked up with a supply of fast-friendly meals on
days when you really don't feel like cooking.

speedy spinach and prawn curry

234

calories per serve (980 kJ)

Serves 1

75 g (2¾ oz/5 medium) peeled and deveined raw prawns (shrimp),
  tails left intact
filtered water, as needed
250 g (9 oz) frozen chopped English spinach, thawed and well drained
250 ml (9 fl oz/1 cup) chicken stock
1 tablespoon coconut cream
2 teaspoons curry powder, or to taste
½ teaspoon ground cumin
Celtic sea salt and freshly ground black pepper, to taste

Put the prawns in a small saucepan with just enough filtered water to cover. Place over medium heat, then bring to a gentle simmer and poach the prawns for 3–4 minutes, until just cooked through.

Meanwhile, put the remaining ingredients in a small frying pan. Place over medium heat and cook for 5 minutes, then reduce the heat to low and cook for a further 7–10 minutes. Remove from the heat, cool a little, then transfer to a blender or food processor and purée until smooth.

Return the mixture to the pan, add the prawns and cook over low heat for 5 minutes, or until warmed through.

SUPERCHARGED TIP

Gently cooking spinach by steaming until wilted, or simmering over low heat in a curry or stew, will allow you to absorb more of the antioxidant carotenoids and therefore to benefit from their anti-inflammatory effects.

DINNER

sautéed scallops with mushrooms and spinach

calories per
serve (749 kJ)

Serves 2

1 teaspoon extra virgin olive oil
200 g (7 oz/10 small) scallops, rinsed and patted dry
Celtic sea salt and freshly ground black pepper, to taste
2 garlic cloves, crushed
140 g (5 oz) mixed mushrooms, whole or sliced
1 teaspoon fresh or dried rosemary
1 teaspoon dried thyme
1 teaspoon dried oregano
200 g (7 oz) baby English spinach leaves
splash of apple cider vinegar
chopped parsley or rosemary sprigs, to serve
lemon wedges, to serve

Heat the oil in a medium frying pan over medium heat. Season the scallops with salt and pepper, sear in the pan for 1–2 minutes on each side, until golden brown, then remove from the pan and set aside.

Add the garlic, mushrooms, rosemary, thyme and oregano to the pan, then cook, stirring frequently, for 5 minutes. Add the spinach and apple cider vinegar, then cook for 1–2 minutes, until the spinach just begins to wilt. Return the scallops to the pan and cook for 1 minute to heat through.

Serve topped with the parsley or rosemary and with lemon wedges on the side.

SUPERCHARGED TIP

Shellfish such as scallops are a beautiful source of fat-soluble vitamins, especially vitamin D. Always buy shellfish extremely fresh from your local fishmonger and eat as soon as possible.

aromatic zucchini curry

135

*calories per
serve (565 kJ)*

Serves 3

For a satisfying meal on the lighter side, this zucchini-based curry is
affordable and is intentionally full of fat-burning spices, which will
help if you're aiming for weight loss during your fast.

4 garlic cloves, crushed
1 teaspoon grated or finely
  chopped ginger
1 tablespoon ground cumin
1 teaspoon ground turmeric
1 teaspoon ground coriander
½ teaspoon chilli powder or
  sliced fresh chilli
1 teaspoon sesame oil
2 kaffir lime leaves
4 zucchini (courgettes), cut
  into batons

filtered water, as needed
250 ml (9 fl oz/1 cup)
  vegetable stock or filtered
  water
80 ml (2½ fl oz/⅓ cup)
  coconut milk
1 tablespoon lime juice
Celtic sea salt and freshly
  ground black pepper, to taste
coriander (cilantro) leaves,
  to serve

In a small bowl, combine the garlic, ginger and spices.

Heat the oil in a medium saucepan over low heat, add the spice mix and
lime leaves, then cook, stirring, for 2–3 minutes to release the flavours. Add
the zucchini and cook for 2 minutes, adding a little water if necessary to
stop it sticking. Add the stock or water, coconut milk and lime juice, then
season with salt and pepper. Bring to the boil, then reduce the heat to
medium–low and simmer for 5 minutes, or until the zucchini is tender and
the sauce has thickened.

Serve topped with the coriander leaves.

one-pan roasted fish and vegetables

249

calories per
serve (1043 kJ)

Serves 4

4 x 120 g (4¼ oz) thick
  white fish fillets (such as
  barramundi or cod)
juice of 1 lemon
Celtic sea salt and freshly
  ground black pepper, to taste
a few rosemary sprigs
a few thyme sprigs
2 brown onions, cut into
  wedges (optional)
4 garlic cloves
2 zucchini (courgettes), thickly
  sliced lengthways
1 small eggplant (aubergine),
  cut into large dice

2 red capsicums (peppers),
  cut into wedges
2 large orange or yellow
  capsicums (peppers), cut
  into large wedges
1 tablespoon extra virgin olive
  oil
2 teaspoons dried oregano
2 teaspoons dried thyme
1 teaspoon ground cumin
½ teaspoon chilli flakes
thin lemon wedges, to serve
  (optional)

Preheat the oven to 200°C (400°F).

Put the fish fillets in a shallow dish and pour over the lemon juice. Season
with salt and pepper, then top the fillets with the rosemary and thyme
sprigs. Cover and set aside at room temperature while you cook the vegies.

Put the vegetables in a roasting tin, season with salt and pepper, then
drizzle over the olive oil and sprinkle with the herbs and spices. Bake for
25–30 minutes, turning halfway through.

Rest the fish fillets on top of the vegetables and cook for a further
12–15 minutes, until the fish is cooked through.

Serve the fillets on top of the vegetables with lemon wedges (if using).

tamari mushroom beef stir-fry

Serves 4

This dish is great served over spiralised carrot or zoodles (see page 212).

1 teaspoon sesame oil
1 red onion, thinly sliced
2 garlic cloves, crushed
2 teaspoons grated ginger
1 green capsicum (pepper), cut into large pieces
1 red capsicum (pepper), cut into large pieces
70 g (2½ oz) button mushrooms, sliced if large
400 g (14 oz) lean beef fillet, cut into strips
splash of wheat-free tamari
chilli flakes or sliced fresh chilli, to taste
2 tablespoons lime juice
coriander (cilantro) leaves, to serve (optional)

Heat the sesame oil in a medium frying pan over medium heat. Add the onion, garlic and ginger, then cook for 2 minutes. Add the capsicums, mushrooms, beef, tamari, chilli and lime juice, then cook, stirring frequently, for 3–4 minutes, until the beef is done to your liking.

Serve topped with the coriander (if using).

SUPERCHARGED TIP

Spare your wallet and your health by avoiding packaged stir-fry sauces at all costs. These 'convenience foods' are devoid of nutrition and almost always filled with questionable additives and refined ingredients, despite any '100% preservative-free' claims. It's also very easy to make your own with wholefood ingredients.

moroccan quinoa chicken

Serves 4

When preparing quinoa, it's really important to rinse it several
times in a fine-mesh sieve to remove the soapy, bitter saponins in
the grains. You can also sprout quinoa for 2 days before cooking to
increase the available nutrients. This dish is wonderful reheated
the next day for lunch. If not fasting, top with some toasted nuts or
seeds, or crumble over some feta or goat's cheese. For a vegetarian
option, you could add tofu strips or white beans.

1 teaspoon extra virgin olive oil
1 brown onion, chopped
2 garlic cloves, crushed
1 red capsicum (pepper),
　cut into large pieces
200 g (7 oz) pumpkin (winter
　squash), peeled and cut
　into large chunks
1 tablespoon ground cumin
½ teaspoon cayenne pepper
　(optional)
2 teaspoons ground coriander
2 teaspoons sweet paprika

50 g (1¾ oz/¼ cup) quinoa,
　rinsed
300 ml (10½ fl oz) chicken
　stock or filtered water
300 g (10½ oz) skinless
　chicken breast fillets, cut
　into strips
100 g (3½ oz/⅔ cup) frozen
　peas
Celtic sea salt and freshly
　ground black pepper, to taste
coriander (cilantro) leaves,
　to serve

Heat the oil in a large frying pan over medium heat. Add the onion and
garlic, then cook for 2–3 minutes, or until softened. Add the capsicum,
pumpkin, spices, quinoa and stock or water. Bring to the boil, then reduce
the heat to low and simmer, covered, for 10 minutes. Add the chicken and
cook for a further 10 minutes, or until the liquid has been absorbed, the
pumpkin is tender and the chicken is cooked through. Add the peas, season
with salt and pepper, then cook for a further 2 minutes.

Serve topped with the coriander.

mint and ginger prawns
with coleslaw

202

*calories per
serve (846 kJ)*

Serves 2

Prawns are a delicious summertime food loaded with protein to fill
you up. In fact, did you know they have approximately the same
amount of protein as chicken or beef, yet half the calories?

1 small carrot, grated
180 g (6¼ oz/¼ small) cabbage, finely shredded
180 g (6¼ oz/¼ small) red cabbage, finely shredded
2 kale leaves, stalks removed, roughly chopped or torn
1 spring onion (scallion), thinly sliced
1 teaspoon extra virgin olive oil
150 g (5½ oz/10 medium) peeled and deveined
   raw prawns (shrimp), tails left intact
mint leaves, to serve

DRESSING
1 teaspoon finely grated lime zest
1 tablespoon lime juice
1 teaspoon grated ginger
1 garlic clove, crushed
2 teaspoons wheat-free tamari
1 teaspoon sesame oil
1 tablespoon finely chopped mint

Combine all the dressing ingredients in a small jar, then seal and shake well.

Combine the carrot, cabbages, kale and spring onion in a serving bowl.

Heat the oil in a medium frying pan over medium heat. Add the prawns
and cook for 1–2 minutes on each side, until cooked through.

Put the prawns on top of the vegetables, pour over the dressing and serve
topped with the mint leaves.

mediterranean green beans

99

*calories per
serve (414 kJ)*

Serves 4

600 g (1 lb 5 oz) green beans,
  trimmed
1 teaspoon extra virgin olive
  oil
4 garlic cloves, crushed
1 red onion, finely chopped
400 g (14 oz) tinned diced
  tomatoes
1 teaspoon dried oregano

1 teaspoon dried thyme
splash of filtered water
90 g (3¼ oz/2 cups) baby
  English spinach leaves,
  roughly chopped
handful of basil, torn
Celtic sea salt and freshly
  ground black pepper, to taste
squeeze of lemon juice

Steam the green beans over a saucepan of boiling water for 3 minutes.

Heat the oil in a medium frying pan over medium heat. Add the garlic and
onion, then cook for 3–4 minutes, until softened. Add the tomatoes, dried
herbs, green beans and water, then cover and cook for 5 minutes. Stir in
the spinach and cook, stirring frequently, for 1–2 minutes, until just wilted.

Top with the basil, season with salt, pepper and lemon juice, and serve.

SUPERCHARGED TIPS

This recipe is lovely with a serve of tuna (77 calories/322 kJ per 95 g)
or a medium soft-boiled egg (63 calories/264 kJ) added on top for
a portion of protein.

Green beans are the perfect low-calorie ingredient to keep in your
freezer. Blanch in boiling water for 2 minutes or steam for 3 minutes
before drying with paper towel and freezing in snaplock bags.

curried carrot soup

129

*calories per
serve (540 kJ)*

Serves 4 (makes about 1.2 litres/41 fl oz)

1 teaspoon extra virgin olive oil
2 brown onions, finely chopped
1 garlic clove, crushed
500 g (1 lb 2 oz) carrots, sliced
2 teaspoons curry powder
1 teaspoon grated ginger
1 litre (35 fl oz/4 cups) vegetable stock or filtered water
60 ml (2 fl oz/¼ cup) coconut milk
Celtic sea salt and freshly ground black pepper, to taste
chopped parsley and mint, to serve

Heat the oil in a large saucepan over medium heat. Add the onions and garlic, then cook for 3–4 minutes, until softened. Add the carrots, curry powder, ginger and stock or water. Bring to the boil, then cover and reduce the heat to low and simmer for 15 minutes, or until the carrot is tender.

Allow to cool a little, then transfer to a blender, add the coconut milk and blend until smooth. Season with salt and pepper.

Serve topped with parsley and mint.

SUPERCHARGED TIP

Don't be afraid to peel carrots. Unlike many skinned vegetables, which have a concentration of nutrients just under the peel, the vitamins and minerals within carrots are more evenly distributed. If you prefer not to peel, you can give them a good scrubbing instead.

salmon and coriander fishcakes

Makes 4

210 g (7½ oz) tinned salmon
  (or use fresh chopped
  salmon)
1 medium egg, lightly whisked
½ small red onion, finely
  chopped
1 tablespoon chopped
  coriander (cilantro)
2 teaspoons chopped chives,
  plus extra to serve

1 teaspoon chilli flakes
2 teaspoons sugar-free
  mustard
Celtic sea salt and freshly
  ground black pepper, to taste
2 tablespoons coconut flour
1 teaspoon coconut oil
lime slices, to serve

Drain the salmon and put in a medium bowl. Remove the bones (or leave them in if you prefer), then mash the flesh with a fork. Add the egg, onion, herbs, chilli flakes, mustard, salt and pepper. Mix well.

Roll the mixture into one big ball, then cover and chill in the freezer for 30 minutes. When you're ready to cook the fishcakes, take the mixture out of the freezer and divide into four. Shape each portion into a fishcake and sprinkle both sides with flour.

Heat the oil in a medium frying pan over medium heat, then cook the fishcakes for 7–10 minutes on each side, until golden brown.

Serve immediately, with chives scattered over and lime slices on the side.

SUPERCHARGED TIP

Try to select sustainable wild-caught salmon, as farmed salmon isn't fed the same diet, giving it a less favourable fatty-acid profile.

mexican chicken and avocado salad

Serves 4

400 g (14 oz) skinless chicken
  breast fillets, cut into smaller
  pieces
½ teaspoon chilli flakes
60 ml (2 fl oz/¼ cup) lime juice
coconut water, as needed
1 garlic clove, crushed
1 teaspoon ground cumin
1 teaspoon sweet paprika
200 g (7 oz) rocket (arugula)

60 g (2¼ oz/about ½ small)
  avocado, cut into dice
½ red onion, thinly sliced
  into rings
150 g (5½ oz/1 cup) cherry
  tomatoes, halved
Celtic sea salt and freshly
  ground black pepper, to taste
coriander (cilantro) leaves, to
  serve (optional)

Put the chicken in a bowl, add the chilli flakes and half the lime juice, then stir to combine. Cover and refrigerate for 1 hour.

Heat a chargrill pan or frying pan over high heat. Add the chicken and cook for 7–8 minutes, turning to cook on all sides and adding coconut water as needed to stop it sticking.

Make a dressing by combining the garlic, spices and remaining lime juice in a large bowl.

Toss the rocket, avocado, onion and tomatoes together then drizzle over the dressing. Serve the chicken on top of the salad, seasoned with salt and pepper and garnished with coriander (if using).

SUPERCHARGED TIP

A perfect avocado should yield slightly to firm but gentle pressure, particularly at the narrow end.

asian chicken zoodles

Serves 2

2 medium zucchini (courgettes)
1 teaspoon extra virgin coconut oil
200 g (7 oz) skinless chicken
   breast fillets, cut into strips
100 g (3½ oz/2 small) carrots,
   cut into fine matchsticks
70 g (2½ oz) mushrooms, sliced
100 g (3½ oz) baby corn
2 spring onions (scallions),
   sliced or curled

2 garlic cloves, crushed
2 teaspoons grated ginger

DRESSING
2 tablespoons wheat-free tamari
1 tablespoon apple cider vinegar
60 ml (2 fl oz/¼ cup) chicken
   stock
stevia, to taste
½ teaspoon chilli flakes

Combine the dressing ingredients in a small bowl and mix well.

Using a spiraliser or mandoline, cut the zucchini into long spaghetti-like strips ('zoodles'). Alternatively, cut it into thin strips using a vegetable peeler or sharp knife. Set aside until the dish is nearly finished.

Heat the oil in a frying pan or wok over medium–high heat. Add the chicken and cook, turning frequently, for 3–4 minutes, then add the remaining ingredients. Cook, stirring frequently, for 2–3 minutes, until the chicken is cooked through and the vegetables are just tender.

Add the dressing and zoodles to the pan, then cook for another 3–5 minutes, until the sauce has thickened and the zucchini is tender.

SUPERCHARGED TIP

Organic meat can be expensive for budgeting households, but to save money you can buy whole organic chickens and joint them yourself. There are plenty of video tutorials online to teach you how. Use the carcass to make your own chicken stock or bone broth.

hearty minestrone soup

Serves 4

1 teaspoon extra virgin
 coconut oil
1 brown onion, finely chopped
2 garlic cloves, crushed
2 small celery stalks, sliced
470 g (1 lb ½ oz) zucchini
 (courgettes), sliced
245 g (8½ oz/4 medium)
 carrots, sliced
100 g (3½ oz) kale, chopped
400 g (14 oz) tinned diced
 tomatoes

1 tablespoon tomato passata
 (puréed tomatoes)
400 g (14 oz) tinned
 chickpeas, rinsed and
 drained
1 litre (35 fl oz/4 cups)
 vegetable stock
60 g (2¼ oz) buckwheat pasta
1 teaspoon dried oregano
Celtic sea salt and freshly
 ground black pepper, to taste
handful of parsley, chopped

Heat the oil in a large saucepan over medium heat. Add the onion and garlic, then cook, stirring frequently, for 3–4 minutes, until the onion is soft and translucent. Add the celery, zucchini, carrots and kale, then cook for another 3–4 minutes. Add the tomatoes, tomato passata, chickpeas and vegetable stock. Bring to the boil, then reduce the heat to low and simmer gently, covered, for 15 minutes. Add the pasta and cook for another 12–15 minutes, or until the pasta is al dente.

Season with salt and pepper, stir through the parsley and serve.

SUPERCHARGED TIP

The available amount of the powerful health compound allicin is increased significantly when garlic is minced or thinly sliced 10 minutes before cooking. Allicin has wonderful antimicrobial effects to boost the immune system.

rocket and salmon midweek omelette

Serves 1

2 medium eggs
½ teaspoon finely grated lemon zest
pinch of ground nutmeg
2 tablespoons almond milk
Celtic sea salt and freshly ground black pepper, to taste
1 teaspoon extra virgin olive oil
50 g (1¾ oz) smoked salmon
100 g (3½ oz) rocket (arugula)

In a small bowl, whisk the eggs with the lemon zest, nutmeg, almond milk, salt and pepper.

Heat the oil in a small frying pan over medium heat. Pour in the egg mixture and cook for 2–3 minutes. When the bottom of the omelette is just cooked, top with the salmon and rocket. Fold the omelette over the filling and cook until the eggs are done to your liking.

SUPERCHARGED TIP

If you don't have the time or inclination to make your own almond milk, most supermarkets have plenty of this delicious dairy substitute. Just be sure that it's free of additives and sugar (which will be listed as fruit concentrates or cane sugar).

wrapped fish peperonata

Serves 4

4 x 120 g (4¼ oz) thick
  white fish fillets (such as
  barramundi or cod)
2 tablespoons lemon juice
Celtic sea salt and freshly
  ground black pepper, to
  taste
2 teaspoons extra virgin olive
  oil
1 brown onion, thinly sliced
2 garlic cloves, crushed
1 red capsicum (pepper),
  cut into strips

1 yellow capsicum (pepper),
  cut into strips
2 medium tomatoes, chopped
150 g (5½ oz) button
  mushrooms, sliced
stevia, to taste
250 ml (9 fl oz/1 cup)
  vegetable stock
1 teaspoon fresh or dried
  thyme, plus extra to serve
  (optional)
1 teaspoon fresh or dried
  oregano
basil leaves, to serve

Preheat the oven to 180°C (350°F) and line a baking tray with a sheet of
baking paper large enough to enclose all the fish fillets (alternatively you
can wrap each fillet separately).

Place the fillets on the prepared tray. Pour over the lemon juice and season
with salt and pepper. Enclose the fish in the baking paper and bake for
15 minutes, or until cooked through.

Meanwhile, heat the oil in a frying pan over medium heat. Add the onion,
garlic, capsicums, tomatoes and mushrooms, then cook for 5 minutes.

Add the stevia, stock, thyme and oregano. Season with salt and pepper
then bring to the boil. Reduce the heat to low and simmer for 5–10 minutes,
until slightly thickened.

Serve the fish topped with the sauce and garnished with the basil and extra
thyme (if using).

scallop and green bean curry

Serves 2

1 teaspoon extra virgin olive
  oil
100 g (3½ oz/6 small) scallops,
  with roe, rinsed and patted dry
Celtic sea salt and freshly
  ground black pepper, to taste
1 brown onion, finely chopped
1 teaspoon curry powder
1 teaspoon grated ginger

125 ml (4 fl oz/½ cup)
  vegetable stock or filtered
  water
125 ml (4 fl oz/½ cup) coconut
  milk
200 g (7 oz) green beans,
  trimmed and halved lengthways
coriander (cilantro) leaves, to
  serve (optional)

Heat the oil in a medium frying pan over medium heat. Season the scallops
with salt and pepper, sear in the pan for 1–2 minutes on each side, until
golden brown, then remove from the pan and set aside.

Add the onion to the pan and cook for 2–3 minutes, until softened. Add the
curry powder and ginger, then fry for a further 2 minutes. Pour in the stock
or water and the coconut milk, then bring to the boil. Reduce the heat to
low, then simmer for 15 minutes, allowing the sauce to thicken. Add the
green beans and cook for a further 3–4 minutes.

Season with salt and pepper, then add the scallops and cook for 1–2 minutes
to heat through. Serve topped with the coriander (if using).

SUPERCHARGED TIP

Always look for coconut milk in BPA-free tins, as this carcinogenic
compound is absorbed by coconut fat. Also avoid thickeners such as
guar gum, which can act like glue in your digestive tract. Try to find
coconut milk made from 100 per cent coconut extract.

zesty lemon chicken with fresh herbs

168

calories per serve (703 kJ)

Serves 4

This simple stovetop meal will make you forget you're fasting. Make extra for a yummy lunch the next day.

1 teaspoon extra virgin olive oil
1 leek, white part only, sliced
2 garlic cloves, crushed
400 g (14 oz) skinless chicken breast fillets, cut into large pieces
finely grated zest and juice of 1 large lemon
200 g (7 oz) cherry tomatoes, halved

handful of thyme, plus extra to serve
handful of rosemary
200 g (7 oz) baby English spinach leaves
½ teaspoon apple cider vinegar
Celtic sea salt and freshly ground black pepper, to taste

Heat the oil in a large frying pan over medium heat. Add the leek and garlic, then cook for 3–4 minutes, until softened. Add the chicken, lemon zest, half the lemon juice and the tomatoes, then cook, stirring regularly, for 10–15 minutes, until the chicken is cooked through.

Add the herbs, spinach and apple cider vinegar, then cook for 1–2 minutes, until the spinach is just wilted. Season with salt and pepper, then serve topped with the extra thyme.

SUPERCHARGED TIP

On non-fasting days, this recipe tastes delicious served over zoodles (see page 212). Throw them in the pan when you add the spinach.

steak with caramelised onions

269

calories per
serve (1126 kJ)

Serves 2

1 teaspoon extra virgin olive oil
2 brown onions, thinly sliced
1 garlic clove, crushed
filtered water, as needed
splash of balsamic vinegar, or splash of apple cider vinegar
   and a few drops liquid stevia
2 x 100 g (3½ oz) lean beef fillet steaks
Celtic sea salt and freshly ground black pepper, to taste
100 g (3½ oz) rocket (arugula)
1 tablespoon lemon juice

Heat the oil in a medium frying pan over medium heat. Add the onions
and garlic, then cook for 4–5 minutes, until softened. Reduce the heat to
medium–low, then cook for a further 15 minutes, stirring and adding a few
drops of filtered water regularly to prevent the onion sticking to the pan.
Add the balsamic vinegar or apple cider vinegar and stevia, then cook for
another 15 minutes, or until the onion is dark golden and caramelised.

Meanwhile, season the steaks with salt and pepper. Heat a chargrill pan or
frying pan over high heat, then cook the steaks for 2 minutes on each side,
or until cooked to your liking.

Divide the rocket between two plates, then season with salt and pepper,
and drizzle over the lemon juice and any steak juices. Place the steaks on
top. Garnish with the caramelised onions or serve them on the side.

garlicky vegie pasta

Serves 2

60 g (2¼ oz) buckwheat pasta
1 teaspoon extra virgin olive oil
1 small red onion, sliced
2 garlic cloves, crushed
125 g (4½ oz) broccoli, cut into small florets
1 red capsicum (pepper), cut into thin strips
2 tablespoons lemon juice
1 tablespoon wheat-free tamari
2 tablespoons vegetable stock or filtered water
100 g (3½ oz) baby English spinach leaves
Celtic sea salt and freshly ground black pepper, to taste
thyme leaves, to serve

Following the packet instructions, cook the buckwheat pasta until al dente.

Meanwhile, heat the oil in a large frying pan over medium heat. Add
the onion and garlic, then cook for 3–4 minutes, until softened. Add the
broccoli, capsicum, lemon juice and tamari, then cook for 3–4 minutes,
adding the stock or water a little at a time to prevent the vegetables
sticking. Add the spinach and cook for 1–2 minutes, until just wilted.

Serve the vegetable mixture over the pasta and scatter over the thyme.

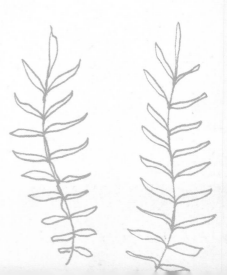

roasted vegetable quinoa

Serves 3

1 medium zucchini (courgette), sliced
1 red capsicum (pepper), cut into thin strips
1 yellow capsicum (pepper), cut into thin strips
1 red onion, sliced
200 g (7 oz) cherry tomatoes, halved
4 garlic cloves, sliced
1 tablespoon extra virgin olive oil
1 tablespoon ground cumin
1 teaspoon ground coriander
pinch of cayenne pepper
65 g (2¼ oz/⅓ cup) quinoa, rinsed
170 ml (5½ fl oz/⅔ cup) vegetable stock or filtered water
100 g (3½ oz) baby English spinach leaves
squeeze of lemon juice
Celtic sea salt and freshly ground black pepper, to taste
2 tablespoons chopped parsley, to serve

Preheat the oven to 200°C (400°F).

Put the zucchini, capsicums, onion, tomatoes and garlic in a roasting tin, drizzle with the olive oil and sprinkle over the spices. Roast for 30 minutes, or until the vegetables are tender, turning halfway through.

Meanwhile, combine the quinoa and stock or water in a small saucepan over medium heat. Bring to the boil, then reduce the heat to low and simmer, covered, for 15 minutes, or until the liquid has been absorbed.

Gently combine the vegetables and quinoa in a large bowl. Divide the spinach between three plates and top with the quinoa mix. Add the lemon juice, season with salt and pepper, then top with the parsley to serve.

fish in a creamy mustard sauce

*calories per
serve (913 kJ)*

Serves 4

Mild-tasting white fish, such as cod or barramundi (which has very high levels of omega-3 fatty acids for a white fish and boasts anti-ageing properties), is beautiful when cooked properly. Ideally, the fish should flake easily and melt in the mouth.

300 g (10½ oz) green beans, trimmed
1 teaspoon extra virgin olive oil
3 spring onions (scallions), thinly sliced
1 garlic clove, finely chopped
4 x 120 g (4¼ oz) firm white fish fillets (such as barramundi or cod)
60 g (2¼ oz/¼ cup) sugar-free wholegrain mustard
125 ml (4 fl oz/½ cup) coconut milk
125 ml (4 fl oz/½ cup) fish stock or filtered water
2 tablespoons chopped parsley, plus extra to serve
Celtic sea salt and freshly ground black pepper, to taste

Put the beans in a large bowl and cover with boiling water. Set aside for 2–3 minutes, then drain and refresh in cold water. Drain and set aside.

Heat the oil in a medium frying pan over medium heat. Add the spring onions and garlic, then cook for 2–3 minutes, until softened. Add the fish fillets, mustard, coconut milk, stock or water and the parsley. Season with salt and pepper, then bring to the boil. Reduce the heat to low and simmer for 10 minutes, until the fish is tender and the sauce has thickened.

Serve with the green beans and extra parsley.

slow-cooker beef stew

Serves 4

400 g (14 oz) lean stewing beef
180 g (6¼ oz/3 medium) carrots, sliced
1 celery stalk, sliced
85 g (3 oz/1 small) sweet potato, scrubbed and sliced
1 red onion, quartered
2 garlic cloves, sliced
250 ml (9 fl oz/1 cup) beef stock or filtered water
2 tablespoons tomato paste (concentrated purée)
2 tablespoons apple cider vinegar
5 thyme sprigs, plus extra to serve
1 bay leaf
6 black peppercorns
Celtic sea salt, to taste

Combine all the ingredients in a slow-cooker and cook on low for 10 hours or high for 4–6 hours. (To cook in a traditional oven, preheat the oven to 160°C/315°F. Combine all the ingredients in an ovenproof casserole dish and cook for 4 hours.)

Discard the thyme sprigs and bay leaf. Serve topped with the extra thyme.

Note: *You can brown off the meat beforehand for a heartier flavour. Brown in 1 teaspoon olive oil (40 extra calories/167 kJ), then add to the slow-cooker with the rest of the ingredients.*

rosemary and thyme chicken stew

267

calories per serve (1118 kJ)

If you're really pressed for time in the evenings, throw all the ingredients in your slow-cooker in the morning and come home to a scrumptious dinner.

Serves 4

145 g (5 oz/2 large) carrots, halved lengthways and sliced
4 small red onions (optional), peeled and quartered
2 leeks, white part only, sliced
2 lemons, quartered
2 garlic cloves
370 g (13 oz/about 2) skinless chicken thighs, halved
625 ml (21½ fl oz/2½ cups) chicken stock

400 g (14 oz) tinned diced tomatoes
2 bay leaves
a few thyme sprigs
a few rosemary sprigs
drizzle of apple cider vinegar
1 teaspoon sugar-free wholegrain mustard
Celtic sea salt and freshly ground black pepper, to taste

~~~~~~~

Preheat the oven to 180°C (350°F).

Put the carrots, onions (if using), leeks, lemons and garlic in a large roasting tin. Rest the chicken thighs on top of the vegetables, then pour in the stock and tomatoes and top with the herbs. Drizzle in the apple cider vinegar, then bake for 35–40 minutes, until the vegetables and chicken are cooked through.

Remove the chicken and vegetables from the pan and keep warm. Discard the bay leaf (and perhaps the lemon quarters if you prefer) and transfer the juices to a saucepan. Bring the juices to the boil, then add the mustard and boil for 5 minutes, or until slightly thickened. Season with salt and pepper.

Pour the sauce over the chicken and vegetables, then serve.

baked fish with leeks and fennel

242

calories per
serve (1013 kJ)

Serves 4

I love experimenting with a fast-friendly protein combined with different seasonal vegies, herbs and spices to make the perfect flavour combo. This tender baked fish is complemented beautifully by calming fennel, cleansing coriander and the sweetness of leeks.

juice of ½ lemon
4 x 120 g (4¼ oz) thick
  white fish fillets (such as
  barramundi or cod)
Celtic sea salt and freshly
  ground black pepper, to taste
1 teaspoon ground cumin
1 tablespoon fennel seeds
400 g (14 oz) fennel bulb,
  leaves reserved, trimmed
  and sliced

3 leeks, white part only, sliced
2 brown onions, sliced
3 garlic cloves, peeled
2 teaspoons extra virgin
  olive oil
1 teaspoon ground coriander
coriander (cilantro) leaves,
  to serve

Preheat the oven to 180°C (350°F) and line a roasting tin with baking paper.

Pour the lemon juice over the fish fillets, season with salt and pepper, and sprinkle over the cumin and the fennel seeds. Cover and refrigerate for 15–30 minutes.

Put the fennel slices, leeks, onions and garlic in the prepared roasting tin. Drizzle over the olive oil, add the ground coriander, and season with salt and pepper. Mix well, then bake for 25 minutes, turning once.

Sit the fish on the vegetables and cook for a further 15 minutes, or until the fish is cooked through. Serve topped with the coriander and fennel leaves.

chicken and cashew stir-fry

263

calories per
serve (1101 kJ)

Serves 4

50 g (1¾ oz/⅓ cup) raw cashew nuts
1 teaspoon extra virgin olive oil
1 brown onion, sliced
2 garlic cloves, crushed
1 teaspoon grated ginger
450 g (1 lb) skinless chicken breast fillets, cut into pieces
410 g (14½ oz/1 large head) broccoli, cut into bite-sized pieces,
   including stems
1 red capsicum (pepper), cut into thin strips
1 tablespoon wheat-free tamari
1 teaspoon chilli flakes
½ teaspoon stevia
splash of filtered water
freshly ground black pepper, to taste
squeeze of lemon juice
chopped coriander (cilantro), to serve

~~~~~~~~~

Toast the cashew nuts in a dry frying pan over medium heat until golden.
Set aside.

Heat the oil in a large frying pan over medium heat. Add the onion, garlic
and ginger, then cook for 3 minutes, stirring frequently. Add the chicken
and cook for 2–3 minutes, until browned. Add the broccoli and capsicum,
then cook for another 2–3 minutes. Add the tamari, chilli flakes, stevia and
water, then cover and cook for a further 4–5 minutes, until the chicken is
cooked through and the vegetables are tender. Add the cashew nuts and
stir to combine.

Season with pepper, squeeze over the lemon juice and top with the
coriander to serve.

TOTALLY
TOTABLE

vegie soup in a jar

Serves 1

The trick with this soup is to mix it with different flavour hits to create new tastes every day. You can change the grated vegies and greens you use in this base recipe according to seasonal availability. Create your own army of jar soups in advance and stash them in the fridge for up to 1 week. You'll need a mason jar, or other heatproof jar with a lid, that holds approximately 440 ml (15½ fl oz).

90

calories (377 kJ) per serve (without flavour hit – see page 238 for flavour hit calorie values)

BASE INGREDIENTS
1 small zucchini (courgette), spiralised or cut into thin strips using a peeler
½ large carrot, spiralised or grated
½ red capsicum (pepper), cut into thin strips
1 spring onion (scallion), sliced
6 snow peas (mangetout), roughly chopped
45 g (1½ oz/1 cup) baby English spinach leaves
1 lemon or lime wedge

TO SERVE
boiling filtered water, to fill
1 tablespoon wheat-free tamari
1 tablespoon apple cider vinegar
coriander (cilantro) leaves (optional)
1 heaped tablespoon of your chosen flavour hit (see page 238)

Put all the base ingredients in the mason jar and take it to work with you. When lunchtime rolls around, unscrew the lid and add boiling filtered water until three-quarters full. Add the tamari and apple cider vinegar, leave to heat through gently and soften the vegetables for 10 minutes, then stir in flavour hit, top with coriander leaves (if using), and eat.

herby flavour hit

24

*calories per
serve (100 kJ)*

Serves 4

finely grated zest and juice
  of 1 lemon
small handful of parsley
  leaves
small handful of basil leaves

small handful of coriander
  (cilantro) leaves
4 thyme sprigs, leaves picked
2 teaspoons extra virgin olive
  oil

thai flavour hit

48

*calories per
serve (201 kJ)*

Serves 6

1 thumb-sized piece of ginger,
  peeled
1 small red chilli, seeds
  removed (optional)
1 teaspoon sesame oil

2 kaffir lime leaves
1 small bunch coriander
  (cilantro), with roots and
  stems included
40 g (1½ oz/¼ cup) cashew nuts

tikka flavour hit

57

*calories per
serve (239 kJ)*

Serves 6

1 finger-sized piece of
  turmeric, peeled
1 thumb-sized piece of ginger,
  peeled
2 garlic cloves
1 teaspoon cumin seeds
½ teaspoon chilli flakes
  (optional, or to taste)

1 small bunch coriander
  (cilantro), stems and roots
  included
juice of 1 lemon
1 tablespoon tomato paste
  (concentrated purée)
40 g (1½ oz/¼ cup) almonds
1 teaspoon extra virgin
  coconut oil

Pulse all the ingredients of your chosen flavour hit to a paste in a food
processor. Store in a small airtight container in the fridge.

Thai (left), Herby (centre)
and Tikka (right) flavour hits

chia, berry and yoghurt dessert in a jar

347

calories per
serve (1453 kJ)

Serves 1

You'll need a 475 ml (16½ fl oz) mason jar or similar
to carry and serve this scrumptious healthy treat.

200 ml (7 fl oz) coconut water
½ teaspoon vanilla bean paste or alcohol-free vanilla extract
pinch of Celtic sea salt
1 teaspoon rice malt (brown rice) syrup
2 tablespoons chia seeds
80 g (2¾ oz/½ cup) berries of your choice
70 g (2½ oz/¼ cup) full-fat plain yoghurt or coconut yoghurt

~~~~~~~~

Combine the coconut water, vanilla, salt and rice malt syrup in
a small bowl, mixing well.

Put the chia seeds in your jar, then pour in the coconut water mixture
and stir well with a fork. Put the lid on the jar and refrigerate for
30 minutes, or overnight.

Once the chia seeds have absorbed all the liquid, top with a layer
of berries and another of yoghurt and take to work with you.
Refrigerate until lunchtime.

avo cargoes

Serves 2

259

calories per
serve for tuna
(1084 kJ)

256

calories per
serve for
chicken
(1072 kJ)

Make this portable lunch recipe – and the following
few recipes – once and eat twice! These meals are
designed to be divided and eaten once for dinner,
then the leftovers taken for workday lunches. If
more than one in the family is fasting, make them
all then divide to help fasting days sail by.

230 g (8 oz) tinned tuna or
  230 g (8 oz) leftover skinless
  roast chicken, chopped
2 teaspoons lemon juice
½ garlic clove, crushed
1 spring onion (scallion), white
  part finely chopped, green
  part sliced or curled and
  reserved to serve

1 teaspoon sweet paprika,
  plus extra to serve
1 teaspoon extra virgin olive oil
Celtic sea salt and freshly
  ground black pepper, to taste
125 g (4½ oz/1 small) avocado
pinch of chilli flakes (optional)

In a bowl, combine the tuna or chicken, lemon juice, garlic, spring onion,
paprika and olive oil. Season with salt and pepper, then use a fork to
combine well and break up the tuna (if using).

Cut the avocado in half and remove the stone, being careful not to break
the avocado itself or the skin – you want to keep this intact for portability.
Scoop out a 1 cm (½ in) layer of avocado with a spoon, mash it and add it
to the tuna or chicken mixture, then spread the mixture into and over both
halves of the avocado, scattering with the reserved spring onion, paprika
and chilli flakes (if using).

Wrap each half securely in plastic wrap and seal in an airtight container
to take to work.

capsicum cups

Serves 2

Assemble these capsicum cups earlier and store them in the fridge,
ready to bake whenever you wish to eat them. Get home from
work, then pop them in the oven while you shake off the work day.

1 teaspoon ghee or extra
  virgin coconut oil
½ small brown onion, finely
  chopped
½ celery stalk, finely chopped
1 teaspoon ground cumin
1 garlic clove, crushed
220 g (7¾ oz/1 cup) cooked
  quinoa
45 g (1½ oz/1 cup) baby English
  spinach leaves, chopped

1 small carrot, grated
1 tomato, chopped
Celtic sea salt and freshly
  ground black pepper, to taste
1 tablespoon nutritional
  yeast flakes
1 large red capsicum (pepper),
  halved lengthways, seeds
  removed
parsley, to serve

Preheat the oven to 180°C (350°F) and line a baking tray with baking paper.

Heat the ghee or oil in a small saucepan over medium heat. Add the onion
and celery, then cook for 5 minutes, or until soft. Add the cumin and garlic,
then cook for 1 minute. Stir in the quinoa, spinach, carrot and tomato, then
cook for a further 5 minutes. Season with salt and pepper, then stir in the
nutritional yeast.

Divide the mixture between the capsicum halves. Place on the prepared
baking tray, touching so they support each other during cooking, and bake
for 30 minutes, or until the capsicum has softened.

To serve immediately, sprinkle the parsley on top. For lunch the next day,
wrap in plastic wrap, then seal in an airtight container to take to work.

guacamole-filled eggs

Serves 4

165

calories per serve (691 kJ)

6 medium eggs
150 g (5½ oz/1 medium) avocado
1 tablespoon lime juice
½ teaspoon Celtic sea salt
1 tablespoon coconut milk
1 tablespoon chopped coriander (cilantro)
½ red chilli, finely chopped, or chilli flakes to taste
1 tablespoon chopped chives or spring onions (scallions)

~~~~~~~~~~

Put the eggs in a medium saucepan and cover with cold water. Bring to a gentle boil over medium heat, then reduce the heat to low and simmer for 11 minutes. Drain and rinse in cold water. Once cool, peel and halve lengthways. Scoop out the cooked yolks and set aside.

Cut the avocado in half lengthways and remove the stone. Scoop the flesh into a bowl then mash roughly using a fork. Use your fingers to break up the cooked egg yolks and add to the mashed avocado. Stir in the lime juice, salt and coconut milk, then the coriander, chilli and chives or spring onions.

Fill each hollow of the hard-boiled egg halves with a generous tablespoonful of the avocado mixture.

Each serve is three egg halves per person. To take to work on a fasting day, wrap each egg half in plastic wrap and seal in an airtight container.

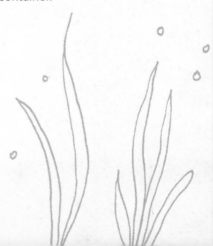

egg-white frittata with silverbeet and herbs

Serves 4

1 teaspoon extra virgin olive oil
1 large leek, white part only, sliced
1 bunch silverbeet (Swiss chard), stalks and ribs removed,
  leaves roughly chopped
2 medium zucchini (courgettes), cut into dice
2 spring onions (scallions), thinly sliced
1 small red capsicum (pepper), sliced
handful of parsley, finely chopped
Celtic sea salt and freshly ground black pepper, to taste
12 medium egg whites, lightly whisked
1 large rosemary sprig, leaves picked

Preheat the oven to 180°C (350°F).

Heat the olive oil in a large frying pan over medium-low heat. Add the
leek and cook for 3–4 minutes, until soft. Add the silverbeet and cook for
2–3 minutes, until wilted. Add the zucchini, spring onions and capsicum,
then cook for a further 2–3 minutes. Stir in the parsley, season with salt and
pepper, then remove from the heat.

Spoon the vegetable mixture into a 28 cm (11¼ in) round quiche dish. Pour
over the egg whites and gently mix into the vegetables. Scatter over the
rosemary leaves.

Bake for 20–25 minutes, or until set and golden.

Cut into quarters to serve. To take to work, wrap each portion in baking
paper or plastic wrap and seal in an airtight container. Eat cold or reheated.

tomato-stuffed zucchini canoes with avocado tahini dressing

103

calories per serve (431 kJ)

Serves 4

2 medium zucchini (courgettes)
2 medium tomatoes, chopped
1 garlic clove, finely chopped
2 teaspoons finely chopped
  parsley
¼ teaspoon dried oregano
2 tablespoons nutritional
  yeast flakes
pinch each of Celtic sea salt
  and freshly ground black
  pepper
salad leaves, to serve (optional)

AVOCADO TAHINI DRESSING
60 g (2¼ oz/½ small) avocado
1 tablespoon tahini
2 tablespoons lemon juice
1 small garlic clove
1 teaspoon extra virgin olive
  oil
pinch each of Celtic sea salt
  and freshly ground black
  pepper

Preheat the oven to 180°C (350°F).

Cut each zucchini in half lengthways, then scoop out the pulp, leaving a 5 mm (¼ in) shell. Chop the pulp and reserve. Put the shells in a steamer over a saucepan of boiling water and cook for 5 minutes, or until just tender.

In a small bowl, combine the zucchini pulp, tomatoes, garlic, parsley, oregano, nutritional yeast, salt and pepper. Spoon into the zucchini shells. Arrange the stuffed shells in a deep baking dish, sitting them close together to support each other, and bake for 20–25 minutes, until cooked through.

Meanwhile, combine the dressing ingredients in a food processor until creamy. Drizzle the dressing over the roasted zucchini boats and serve immediately, with salad leaves (if using).

To take to work, wrap each left-over stuffed zucchini half in plastic wrap, seal in an airtight container in the fridge. Refrigerate the dressing in a separate container and add when ready to eat.

vegie nori wraps

Serves 2

1 tablespoon wheat-free tamari
2 teaspoons rice malt (brown rice) syrup
2 nori sheets
1 tablespoon nut butter (cashew nut butter works well)
a few handfuls of baby English spinach leaves
40 g (1½ oz/½ cup) shredded red cabbage
½ large carrot, grated
100 g (3½ oz/about ½ large) avocado, sliced
small handful of coriander (cilantro), chopped

Combine the tamari and rice malt syrup in a small bowl.

Lay one of the nori sheets on a clean work surface with a long side facing
you and the shiny side down, then evenly spread half the nut butter over it,
leaving a 3 cm (1¼ in) border on the top side. Spread about one-third of the
tamari mixture over the nut butter. Spread a tiny bit of tamari on the top
side to help the wrap stay rolled up. Put your desired amount of spinach
on top of the nut butter and tamari layers, followed by half of each of the
remaining ingredients. Be sure not to pile on *too* much or the wrap could
break when you roll it up. Roll the nori up away from you until sealed.

Cut into three. Repeat with the remaining ingredients.

Wrap in plastic wrap, seal in an airtight lunchbox and refrigerate until
ready to eat.

Note: *Feel free to add or substitute any additional fresh vegies you like!*

bento box

Serves 1

This is easiest to eat from a bento box or lunchbox with four separate sections. Once assembled, refrigerate for lunch the following day.

sesame slaw with tahini and orange dressing

15 g (½ oz/¼ cup) shredded
  green cabbage
15 g (½ oz/¼ cup) shredded
  red cabbage
40 g (1½ oz/¼ cup) grated carrot
a few mint stalks, chopped
a few parsley stalks, chopped
1 tablespoon finely chopped
  spring onion (scallion)
1 tablespoon sesame seeds,
  toasted in a dry frying pan

DRESSING
2 tablespoons lemon juice
1 teaspoon extra virgin olive oil
1 teaspoon tahini
finely grated zest of ½ orange
6 drops liquid stevia
Celtic sea salt and freshly
  ground black pepper, to taste

~~~~~~

Combine all the slaw ingredients except the sesame seeds and put in a section of the box. Combine the dressing ingredients, adding filtered water as needed, then pour over the salad. Top with the sesame seeds.

sardines with lemon and pepper

45 g (1½ oz) tinned sardines
freshly ground black pepper,
  to taste
1 lemon wedge

~~~~~~

Drain the sardines and place in a section of your box. Season with pepper and add the lemon wedge.

zesty quinoa

110 g (4¼ oz/½ cup)
  cooked quinoa
finely grated zest of 1 lime
Celtic sea salt and freshly
  ground black pepper, to taste

~~~~~~

Combine the quinoa and lime zest, then season with salt and pepper. Transfer to a section of your box.

sweet treat

Put a small handful of berries in the last section of the box for dessert.

stuffed sweet potatoes

Serves 2

The additional toppings are for two people.

125 g (4½ oz/2 very small) sweet
  potatoes, skin scrubbed
1 teaspoon ghee
60 g (2¼ oz/about ½ small)
  avocado
juice of 1 lemon
Celtic sea salt and freshly
  ground black pepper, to taste
100 g (3½ oz/½ cup) tinned
  red kidney beans, rinsed and
  drained

ADDITIONAL TOPPINGS
2 tablespoons finely chopped
  red onion
2 tablespoons diced tomato

1 large carrot, grated
2 tablespoons finely chopped
  coriander (cilantro)
2 tablespoons sliced spring
  onion (scallion)
2 tablespoons sprouts (snow
  pea/mangetout, alfalfa,
  broccoli)
60 g (2¼ oz/1⅓ cups) baby
  English spinach leaves, chopped
100 g (3½ oz/1 cup) julienned
  snow peas (mangetout)
½ teaspoon chilli flakes
½ teaspoon smoked paprika
1 tablespoon nutritional
  yeast flakes

Preheat the oven to 200°C (400°F).

Prick the sweet potatoes with a fork a few times, then put on a baking tray and roast for 35–45 minutes, depending on their size. You'll know they're done when the skin is soft and you can pierce the flesh easily with a knife. Allow to cool slightly, then slice each lengthways down the centre, almost to the bottom, and put half the ghee in each cut.

Blend the avocado and lemon juice until smooth, then season with salt and pepper. Stuff the slit in the sweet potatoes with the kidney beans, a dollop of creamy avocado and your choice of additional toppings.

Allow to cool, then wrap each sweet potato in plastic wrap, seal in an airtight container and refrigerate until you take them to work.

lettuce wraps with lamb mince

Serves 4

1 teaspoon extra virgin
  coconut oil
1 large brown onion, finely
  chopped
2 garlic cloves, crushed
1 teaspoon ground cinnamon
¾ teaspoon Celtic sea salt
¼ teaspoon freshly ground
  black pepper
180 g (6¼ oz) lean minced
  (ground) lamb
handful of parsley, chopped

100 g (3½ oz/½ cup) chopped
  tomato
90 g (3¼ oz/½ cup) chopped
  Lebanese (short) cucumber
8 large cos (romaine) lettuce
  leaves
70 g (2½ oz/¼ cup) full-fat
  plain yoghurt
60 g (2¼ oz/about ½ small)
  avocado, mashed
2 tablespoons torn mint leaves
1 tablespoon pine nuts, toasted

Heat a large frying pan over high heat. Add the oil and swirl to coat. Add
the onion, garlic, cinnamon, salt, pepper and lamb, then cook, stirring
frequently, for 5 minutes, or until the lamb is cooked.

Combine the parsley, tomato and cucumber in a medium bowl, then stir in
the lamb mixture.

When ready to eat, put about ¼ cup of the lamb mixture in each lettuce
leaf, then top with yoghurt, avocado, mint and pine nuts. Wrap in plastic
wrap and refrigerate until you take to work.

tahini and cauliflower mash in a flask

Serves 2

Make your vacuum-flask meals the night before, then flask up in the morning ready for the work day ahead. Wrap them in a tea towel to keep them warm until lunchtime. A flask is your fast friend!

575 g (1 lb 4½ oz/1 medium) cauliflower, cut into florets
2 garlic cloves, crushed (omit if you share an office!)
1 tablespoon tahini
2 teaspoons extra virgin olive oil or ghee
1 teaspoon ground cumin
juice of 1 lemon
raw vegie sticks, to serve

Put the cauliflower florets in a steamer over a saucepan of boiling water and cook, covered for 12–15 minutes, until tender – the florets can be verging on soft but shouldn't be falling apart.

Roughly mash the cauliflower with the remaining ingredients, except the vegie sticks, or transfer the cauliflower to a blender or food processor and blend with all the other ingredients until smooth.

Heat half the mash in a small saucepan over medium heat, then seal in your vacuum flask ready for work. Wrap in a tea towel (dish towel) to keep warm until lunchtime. Take some raw vegie sticks along with you. Refrigerate the remainder and reheat for your vaccuum flask the following day.

Flask meals: Smoked Paprika
Meatball Soup (top), Tahini
and Cauliflower Mash (above)
and Chicken and Edamame
Clear Soup (left)

smoked paprika meatball soup in a flask

Serves 6

½ large red capsicum
  (pepper), cut into fine dice
½ red onion, cut into fine dice
4 garlic cloves, crushed
6 small green or black olives,
  pitted and sliced
1 small green chilli, seeds
  removed, finely chopped
450 g (1 lb) lean minced
  (ground) lamb, beef or pork
1 medium egg
30 g (1 oz/¼ cup) coconut flour
1 tablespoon smoked paprika

Celtic sea salt and freshly
  ground black pepper, to taste
100 g (3½ oz/1 medium) sweet
  potato, cut into large dice
1.125 litres (39 fl oz/4½ cups)
  beef stock
400 g (14 oz) tinned diced
  tomatoes
1 teaspoon coconut oil
filtered water, as needed
3 kale leaves, stalks removed,
  roughly chopped
splash of wheat-free tamari

Combine the capsicum, onion, garlic, olives and chilli in a large bowl. Add the meat, egg, coconut flour, paprika, salt and pepper, then mix thoroughly using your hands. Shape the mixture into golf-ball-sized meatballs.

Put the sweet potato, stock and tomatoes in a large saucepan over medium heat and bring to a simmer.

Meanwhile, heat the oil in a large frying pan over medium–high heat, then cook the meatballs, turning frequently, until they have a nice brown crust. Add the meatballs to the simmering liquid. Deglaze the frying pan with a little of the simmering liquid, scraping all the yummy bits off the bottom, then return to the pan. Simmer the meatballs, covered, for 15 minutes, or until cooked through. Add the kale halfway through. When the meatballs are cooked, add the tamari and season with salt and pepper.

Serve immediately for dinner or refrigerate for later. Heat a portion in a small saucepan over medium heat then seal in your vacuum flask for work.

chicken and edamame clear soup in a flask

106

calories per serve (444 kJ)

Serves 6

400 g (14 oz) skinless chicken breast fillets, chopped or sliced
60 g (2¼ oz/1 cup) shelled edamame
1 litre (35 fl oz/4 cups) chicken stock
2 teaspoons wheat-free tamari, plus extra as needed
juice of 1 lemon, plus extra as needed
1 tablespoon apple cider vinegar, plus extra as needed
stevia, to taste
90 g (3¼ oz/¾ cup) raw zoodles (zucchini/courgette noodles,
  see page 212), made using a spiraliser or peeler
2 tablespoons chopped spring onion (scallion)

Combine the chicken, edamame, stock, tamari, lemon juice and vinegar in a large saucepan over medium heat and bring to the boil. Reduce the heat to low and simmer, covered, for 12 minutes. Add the stevia, and adjust the flavour with tamari, lemon juice and apple cider vinegar if necessary.

If eating immediately, remove portions to refrigerate for later, then add the right portions of zoodles and spring onion to the pan and cook for 3 minutes. To take a saved portion to work, warm one portion in a small saucepan over medium heat and add one-sixth of the zoodles and spring onion to the pan. Cook for 3 minutes, then pour into your vacuum flask and seal. Wrap in a tea towel (dish towel) to keep warm until lunchtime.

NOTES

How intermittent fasting works

p. 14   Scientific research into intermittent fasting ...: J.E. Brown et al., 'Intermittent fasting: a dietary intervention for prevention of diabetes and cardiovascular disease?', *British Journal of Diabetes and Vascular Disease*, March/April 2013, vol. 13, no. 2, pp. 68–72.

The health benefits of intermittent fasting

p. 19   Studies on mice have shown that periods ...: University of Southern California, 'Fasting triggers stem cell regeneration of damaged, old immune system', *Science Daily*, 5 June 2014, www.sciencedaily.com/releases/2014/06/140605141507.htm.

p. 19   Dietary restriction has been shown ...: B. Martin et al., 'Caloric restriction and intermittent fasting: Two potential diets for successful brain aging', *Ageing Research Reviews*, 2006, vol. 5, no. 3, pp. 332–53.

Tips to starting your first fast

p. 31   Journalling can profoundly improve your wellbeing ...: P.M. Ullrich & S.K. Lutgendorf, 'Journaling about stressful events: effects of cognitive processing and emotional expression', *Annals of Behavioral Medicine*, 2002, vol. 24, no. 3, pp. 244–50, see transformationalchange.pbworks.com/f/stressjournaling.pdf.

Intermittent fasting and exercise

p. 36   Research shows that exercising on an empty stomach ...: K. Van Proeyen et al., 'Beneficial metabolic adaptations due to endurance exercise training in the fasted state', *Journal of Applied Physiology* (1985), 2011, vol. 110, no. 1, pp. 236–45.

p. 38   Studies show that combining fasting with HIIT triggers …:
M. Esbjörnsson, 'Sprint exercise enhances skeletal muscle p70S6k
phosphorylation and more so in women than in men', *Acta Physiologica*,
2012, vol. 205, no. 3, pp. 411–22.

Slowing down cravings during fasting

p. 43   Research from Dr Jon May and his team …: J. Skorka-Brown et al.,
'Playing Tetris decreases drug and other cravings in real world settings',
Addictive Behaviors, 2015, vol. 51, pp. 165–70.

p. 46   A study published in *Psychology and Health* in 2012 …: R. Moffitt et al.,
'A comparison of cognitive restructuring and cognitive defusion as
strategies for resisting a craved food', *Psychology and Health*, 2012,
vol. 27, supplement no. 2, pp. 74–90.

Portion control

p. 67   Research has proven that larger plates …: B Wansink & K. van Ittersum,
'The visual illusions of food: why plates, bowls, and spoons can bias
consumption volume', *FASEB Journal*, 2006, vol. 20, no. 4, p. A618.

Weight loss and influential foods

p. 79   A study in obese men …: K.M. Liau et al., 'An open-label pilot study to
assess the efficacy and safety of virgin coconut oil in reducing visceral
adiposity', *ISRN Pharmacology*, 2011, article no. 949686, www.ncbi.nlm.
nih.gov/pmc/articles/PMC3226242.

p. 80   Chillies, chilli flakes and cayenne pepper contain …: F. Kawabata et al.,
'Non-pungent capsaicin analogs (capsinoids) increase metabolic rate and
enhance thermogenesis via gastrointestinal TRPV1 in mice', *Bioscience,
Biotechnology, and Biochemistry*, 2009, vol. 73, no. 12, pp. 2690–97.

p. 80   A randomised, double-blind crossover study of walnut . . .: A.M. Brennan
et al., 'Walnut consumption increases satiation but has no effect on
insulin resistance or the metabolic profile over a 4-day period', *Obesity*
(Silver Spring), 2010, vol. 18, no. 6, pp. 1176–82.

p. 83   Studies on overweight mice show that garlic …: M.S. Lee et al.,
'Reduction of body weight by dietary garlic is associated with an
increase in uncoupling protein mRNA expression and activation of
AMP-activated protein kinase in diet-induced obese mice', *Journal of
Nutrition*, 2011, vol. 141, no. 11, pp. 1947–53.

INDEX